PENGUIN BOOKS

Under Milk Wood

Dylan Marlais Thomas was born in 1914 in Swansea. His father was senior English master at the Grammar School, where Dylan Thomas received his only formal education before becoming for eighteen months a reporter on the local newspaper. His early poetry matured quickly in private notebooks, and 1934 saw the publication of the twenty-year-old's first volume, *18 Poems*. Thereafter, bohemian literary life in London alternated with more positively creative periods back in Wales, but his London reputation also laid the base for a celebrated career in the 1940s and early 1950s as a writer for radio and film. Meanwhile, his second and third volumes – *Twenty-five Poems* (1936) and *The Map of Love* (1939) – consolidated his standing as a poet. In 1937 he married Caitlin Macnamara and in 1938 settled for the first time in Laugharne, the Carmarthenshire seaside village now most closely associated with his name, and a profound influence on his final works. Even at the end of the 1930s, holiday memories of rural Carmarthenshire joined native urban memories of Swansea in the autobiographical short stories of *Portrait of the Artist as a Young Dog* (1940). The relatively few poems written during the war years are still among the finest anti-war poems of the century; and 1944–5, spent partly at New Quay on the Cardiganshire coast, was an *annus mirabilis* of remembrances of childhood in poetry and prose. *Deaths and Entrances* in 1946 confirmed his status as a major lyric poet.

Between 1946 and 1949, with proximity to London for film and broadcasting work, the family lived in or near Oxford. 1949 saw a return to Laugharne, to the now famous Boat House. From 1950 on, the poet's attention was given mainly to completing *Under Milk Wood*, a 'Play for Voices' that had grown out of his work for radio and film, and from his experience of New Quay and Laugharne. His growing renown led to four lecturing tours of the United States, where a collection of late poems, *In Country Sleep*, was published in 1952. The same year saw the publication of his *Collected Poems 1934–1952*, to wide acclaim. *Under Milk Wood* received its first readings with actors at the Poetry Center of the Young Men's and Young Women's Hebrew Association in New York in May and October 1953. Dylan Thomas died in New York on 9 November

7516/99

from excessive drinking and medical mistreatment. He is buried at Laugharne.

Walford Davies was educated at the University of Oxford and was formerly Senior Lecturer in English Literature at St Anne's College, Oxford. He holds a personal chair in English Literature of the University of Wales and is currently Visiting Professor of English at the University of Rio Grande, Ohio.

He is the author of two critical studies of Dylan Thomas (*Dylan Thomas*, Open University Press, 1986 and *Dylan Thomas*, University of Wales Press, 1990). Amongst other volumes, he has edited (for Dent, unless otherwise stated): *Dylan Thomas: Early Prose Writings* (1971), *New Critical Essays* (1972), *Wordsworth: Selected Poems* (1974), *Gerard Manley Hopkins: The Major Poems* (1979), *Thomas Hardy: Selected Poems* (1982), *Dylan Thomas: The Collected Stories* (1983), *Deaths and Entrances* (Gregynog Press, 1984), *Dylan Thomas: Selected Poems* (1993), *Gerard Manley Hopkins: Poetry and Prose* (1999), and, with Ralph Maud, *Dylan Thomas: Collected Poems 1934–1953* (1988) and *Under Milk Wood* (1995).

The present new edition of *Under Milk Wood* is a companion volume to Walford Davies's new Penguin edition of Dylan Thomas's *Selected Poems*.

DYLAN THOMAS

Under Milk Wood

A PLAY FOR VOICES

Edited with an Introduction and Notes by Walford Davies

PENGUIN BOOKS

PENGUIN BOOKS

Published by the Penguin Group
Penguin Books Ltd, 80 Strand, London WC2R 0RL, England
Penguin Putnam Inc., 375 Hudson Street, New York, New York 10014, USA
Penguin Books Australia Ltd, 250 Camberwell Road, Camberwell, Victoria 3124, Australia
Penguin Books Canada Ltd, 10 Alcorn Avenue, Toronto, Ontario, Canada M4V 3B2
Penguin Books India (P) Ltd, 11 Community Centre, Panchsheel Park, New Delhi – 110 017, India
Penguin Books (NZ) Ltd, Cnr Rosedale and Airborne Roads, Albany, Auckland, New Zealand
Penguin Books (South Africa) (Pty) Ltd, 24 Sturdee Avenue, Rosebank 2196, South Africa

Penguin Books Ltd, Registered Offices: 80 Strand, London WC2R 0RL, England

www.penguin.com

First published by Dent, 1954

Published in Penguin Classics 2000

8

Set in 10/12.5pt PostScript Monotype Garamond
Typeset by Rowland Phototypesetting Ltd,
Bury St Edmunds, Suffolk
Printed in England by Clays Ltd, St Ives plc

Contents

Acknowledgements

My main debt is to Ralph Maud with whom I had the pleasure of collaborating on the 1995 Dent edition of *Under Milk Wood*, as previously on the Dent edition of the *Collected Poems 1934–1953* in 1988. My debt is also great to John Carey and Christopher Ricks for their teaching and example, and to Paul Ferris, Gilbert Bennett and Jeff Towns for ready advice and information. I thank them all also for their friendship.

Once again thanks are due to the Beinecke Rare Book and Manuscript Library of Yale University Library; the Bodleian Library, Oxford; the Department of Manuscripts of the British Library; the Harry Ransom Humanities Research Center of the University of Texas; and the Rosenbach Museum and Library, Philadelphia. I am also grateful to the British Academy for grants in aid of research.

Introduction

'There is something in the house that prevents his feeling funny.'
(Algernon Blackwood, 'John Silence')

We can still laugh with the dead, but to laugh with living writers is, on the whole, a serious undertaking. And if anybody listening is reserving the writing of his comic book for a rainy day, then what does he think this is? — the dry spring of the world?
(Dylan Thomas, 'A Dearth of Comic Writers')

Under Milk Wood opens, famously, with 'To begin at the beginning'. The beginning is the 'darkest-before-dawn' night in which we hear the fantasy dreams of the inhabitants of a small Welsh seaside town. Dylan Thomas said that he loved small towns by the sea, and small towns by the sea in Wales best of all. *Under Milk Wood*'s beginning starts a one-day cycle in which we later follow the activities of the characters, as fantastic as their dreams, through the morning, afternoon and into the second night of this 'town that never was' until, in the equally striking final sentence of the play, 'the suddenly wind-shaken wood springs awake for the second dark time this one Spring day'.

It makes sense to begin at the beginning. But it is in the middle that any introduction to this brilliant 'play for voices' must start. Not the middle of the play but of Dylan Thomas's career. As things turned out, it was also the middle of his short mature life. The poet who came to prominence early out of Wales at the age of twenty in 1934 also died early in New York at the age of thirty-nine in 1953. Twenty years (1914–1934) went to his making as the son of the Senior English Master at Swansea Grammar School. Both his parents were Welsh-speaking products of late nineteenth-century rural Carmarthenshire. But Dylan was a born 'townee', a product of business–industrial Swansea, a town he later dubbed, in tribute to both James Joyce and himself, 'little Dublin'. His own urban background helped sharpen his enjoyment of the pastoral possibilities of the play. Only another twenty years (1934–1953) remained to him to express in poem, short story, essay, broadcast, filmscript, and *Under Milk Wood* itself (only just finished before his death) the particular nature of his vision. It is in the middle of that career, around 1944–5, that it is best to start.

Yet it was right to echo first of all his famous injunction to 'begin at the beginning'. Thomas's poems are always good on beginnings:

> In the beginning was the three-pointed star,
> One smile of light across the empty face . . .

> Awake my sleeper, to the sun,
> A worker in the morning town . . .

> Myself to set foot
> That second
> In the still sleeping town and set forth.

That first quotation (1933) reminds us that 'to begin at the beginning' is biblical, with a hint of the Holy Ghost of Genesis moving 'on the face of the waters'. Along with 'empty face' we also hear the 'empty space' of Creation, and later it was indeed an empty space – of the airwaves of radio (then more vividly called the 'wireless') – that *Under Milk Wood* as a play for voices sought to cross and fill. In those pre-television days, 'Let there be sound' retained some of the wonder of 'Let there be light'. Even as late as 1950, Thomas in a broadcast was still amazed to be speaking across 'this, to me, unbelievable lack of wires'. And the distinguished broadcaster Alistair Cooke recently recalled even a national difference in this amazement: in Britain in the 1940s, he said, radio listeners leaned forward, when in a technologically more sophisticated America they leaned back. In the second quotation (1934) the Swansea twenty-year-old tells himself to shake off his teenage lethargy and spring awake like a town at the start of a new day. It is with that same energy that *Under Milk Wood* pictures a small community coming with boast and bustle into morning life: 'Llareggub this snip of a morning is wildfruit and warm, the streets, fields, sands and waters springing in the young sun.' And the third quotation (1944) already suggests the lonely spectator, detached from the life of a small community, able to look in from the outside, night or day.

But these are poems, and the poems are strangely unpeopled. There, Thomas's song is ultimately of himself. The great strength of *Under Milk Wood*, his only play and now his best-known work, is the Chaucerian life and liveliness of its sixty or more characters, enjoyed in all their spontaneous eccentricity. And yet the play is obviously written by the same poet. It shares with the poetry that vision of innocence that makes things seem as if self-born, born anew. In the play, Thomas said, all was to be 'strangely simple and simply strange'. He is very good on beginnings.

But of course, in T. S. Eliot's words, our beginnings never know our ends. But Thomas is also powerful on endings. The title of his greatest single volume of poetry is *Deaths and Entrances* (1946), entrances *and* deaths. He decided on the title six years before its publication: 'that is all I ever write about', he said to Vernon Watkins in 1940, 'or want to write about'. But he meant both deaths and entrances. In the famous 'Fern Hill' (1945), we remember that 'as I was young and easy in the mercy of his means,/ Time held me green and dying/ Though I sang in my chains like the sea'. But that 'held me' is itself held between 'mercy' and 'chains', suggesting *cradles me* as well as *enchains me*. And in *Under Milk Wood*, too, endings and beginnings are celebrated together – not just taken for granted but *celebrated*. With a wonderfully literal understanding of the word 'creature' (that which has been 'created') as well as of its role as cliché ('poor creature'), the Reverend Eli Jenkins prays in his evening hymn at the end of the play:

> O please to keep Thy lovely eye
> On all poor creatures born to die

– while playing also on 'lovely', one of the great optimistic words of the depressed South Wales valleys. 'Born to die', then: beginnings *and* endings. *Under Milk Wood* is good on both. By starting in the middle of Thomas's writing career, it is possible to see why this is so.

The aim of the play is obviously to make us laugh. But as with all good comedy since Chaucer's *Canterbury Tales* or Shakespeare's plays, our laughter is never thoughtless. In a 1948 broadcast Thomas quoted one of Algernon Blackwood's 'John Silence' stories in which the wife of a comic writer says that 'There is something in the house that prevents his feeling funny.' The point is that the comedy of *Under Milk Wood* has a strong moral impulse (moral, not moralistic – that is a different thing). The play grew from a period of tragedy, a good while before Thomas actually started writing it. During the Second World War he was deeply appalled by the war's display of man's inhumanity to man. He spent a good part of the war years in London, working for radio and film, and was profoundly demoralized by the effects of the German bombing raids on the city, especially in the Blitz of 1940–41. It is odd still to hear that this was a period in which some careerists 'had a good war'! A BBC internal memo of 12 December 1940 describes Thomas's shocked state at BBC's Broadcasting House after the previous night's incendiary raids, raids that had demolished even more comprehensively his birth-town, Swansea. On the morning following the third and worst Swansea raid, he and his wife Caitlin are recorded painfully picking their way through the rubble. But later, people had to face the even more demoralizing facts of Nazi genocide and the obscene atrocities of the concentration camps. And all this was finally stopped only by means of yet another kind of atrocity, the dropping of the atomic bombs on Hiroshima and Nagasaki. Almost all Dylan Thomas's writing after 1945 took as theme, directly or indirectly, a search to confirm again the possibility of innocence. That is the sense in which the laughter behind *Under Milk Wood* isn't thoughtless. The play needs – not deserves, but needs – to see itself as 'a greenleaved sermon on the innocence of men'.

Outlining a plan for a long poem to be called 'In Country Heaven', set in a post-holocaust period, Thomas said that 'The Earth has killed itself. It is black, petrified, wizened, poisoned, burst; insanity has blown it rotten; and no creatures at all shortly and brutishly hunt their days down like enemies on that corrupted face . . . And the poem becomes, at last, an affirmation of the beautiful and terrible worth of the Earth.' The echo of Thomas Hobbes's *Leviathan* ('No arts; no letters; no society; and which is worst of all, continual fear and danger of violent death;

and the life of man solitary, poor, nasty, brutish, and short') is not accidental. And of 'Poem on his Birthday', contemporary with the completion of *Under Milk Wood* in 1953, Thomas said that it concerns a poet 'progressing, afraid, to his own fiery end in the cloud of an atomic explosion'. This is the climate of fear, only recently lessened in the 1990s by the rearrangement of world power, in which *Under Milk Wood* was written. It now seems not only significant but sad that for his second visit to America in 1952, when he was busily writing the play, Thomas had trouble even obtaining a visa – only because three years earlier he had accepted an invitation as guest of the Czech government to visit Prague to mark the inauguration of the Czechoslovak Writers' Union. To call this the 'Cold War' belies the warmth of all people of imaginative sympathy who lived through it and thought it obscene.

Because of his early death, Thomas seems to us now to have moved even more quickly than others from birth (at the outbreak of the Great War) through a precocious poetic maturity in the 1930s (itself a decade of social collapse and rumours of another war) to a Second World War of even worse horrors and a still darkening aftermath. But his artistic development, like that of Keats, did have this driven quality. The idea that a small seaside community, for all its sins and foibles, could still 'spring awake for the second dark time this one Spring day' – or spring awake at all – held for him a genuinely thankful wonder, 'if only for a last time', as he put it in the poem 'Holy Spring' in 1944. A sense of innocence, beyond the reach of bureaucrats or politicians or soldiers, was something the imagination had to fight for. At such times, memories of childhood come centre-stage. Of the demolition of Swansea by German bombs in 1941 Thomas, significantly conflating place and person, could only say 'our childhood is dead'. And in 1943–5 he was writing, not only the great odes to childhood, 'Poem in October' and 'Fern Hill', but also 'Reminiscences of Childhood' and 'A Child's Christmas in Wales' for radio, and the filmscript 'Twenty Years A-Growing', based on Maurice O'Sullivan's classic autobiography of a luminous childhood on the Blasket Islands.

This last was written at New Quay, a small fishing village on the Cardiganshire coast which, like Laugharne, was to provide exquisite material for the atmosphere and human eccentricity of the 'place of love' he finally called Llareggub. Like our laughter, the lyrical remembrance of things past wasn't thoughtless. He said, with a bluntness kinder than at first appears, that there is only one thing worse than having had an unhappy childhood, and that is to have had a happy one. The need to recapture the happy childhood he himself had had was no case of simple nostalgia. It was to remember, in George Eliot's words, that 'we could never have loved the earth so well, if we had had no childhood in it'. This is the feeling that floods also through the play. One critic thought it odd that 'Fern Hill' should have been written in 1945, because he found it about 'as political as a mountain goat'. But everything 'political' doesn't have to be spelt out. This is certainly true of *Under Milk Wood*. The town so wittily called Llareggub is clearly not about buggerall.

But *Under Milk Wood* is not only 'a place of love'. It is quintessentially 'A Play for Voices'. Its sharp specialist techniques were those learnt in a broadcasting system that survived the war as a democratic public service. It is ironic as well as poignant, then, that Thomas wrote at Laugharne on the very eve of that war a poem that opens yet again with the idea of a small town waking to a new day and dispelling the dreams of night:

> When I woke, the town spoke . . .
>
> I heard, this morning, waking,
> Crossly out of the town noises
> A voice in the erected air . . .
> Cry my sea town was breaking.

For the 'voice in the erected air' was, of course, that of a wireless, the radio. The medium which on 3 September 1939 carried prime minister Neville Chamberlain's declaration that 'As from 11 o'clock today, this country is at war with Germany' was the very medium that, the other side of the war, would carry the indirect protest of the 'play for voices' against all such madness.

But some of the techniques that make the play arguably the best dramatic piece ever written for radio had been exercised much further back even than Thomas's first work for that medium, in some cases even further back than 1939. Yet a crucial insight certainly did strike

Thomas in 1939. Married and with his first child on the way, he had newly settled in Laugharne, the village in south-west Wales that became the main inspiration for the play. In December 1939, as part of a 'Laugharne Entertainment' in aid of the Red Cross, Thomas, the novelist Richard Hughes, author of *A High Wind in Jamaica*, Hughes's wife Frances and Mr Gleed the local butcher took part in a one-act farce, *The Devil Among the Skins* by Ernest Goodwin. Reflecting on the experience, Thomas told Richard Hughes: 'What Laugharne really needs is a play about well-known Laugharne characters – and get them all to play themselves.' This idea that the locals are already dramatic enough is the very heart of *Under Milk Wood*. It was also uncannily prescient: during the war years, several films – *The Silent Village* in 1943, for example – also had villagers playing themselves. In an unpublished 1937 letter to a girlfriend Thomas wrote, with a concern all the more convincing for its privacy, that 'the only democratic conception of human equality is that all men are tragic and comic: we die; we have noses. We are not united by our drabness and smallness, but by our heroisms; the common things are wonderful; the drab things are those that are not common.' It is a typically Chaplinesque insight: we have to invert our sense of heroism, otherwise little Hitlers come to power. At that time, Thomas was writing the comic short stories about his own birthplace Swansea in his satirical but forgiving autobiography, *Portrait of the Artist as a Young Dog* (1940). Comic local colour was obviously something seriously to hang on to.

But some of the techniques that give us not only 'characters' but a bird's-eye view of them went back even further. Thomas's earliest prose works had been full of items that could, with only a slight shift in tone, take their place in the later play. Everyone now knows this exchange in *Under Milk Wood*:

MR OGMORE

I must put my pyjamas in the drawer marked pyjamas.

MR PRITCHARD

I must take my cold bath which is good for me.

MR OGMORE

I must wear my flannel band to ward off sciatica.

MR PRITCHARD

I must dress behind the curtain and put on my apron.

But it was prefigured in a piece Thomas wrote for his school magazine:

MUSSOLINI

Is nothing in this place ever right?

WIFE [*complacently*]

No dear. I hope you remembered to change your underclothing.

MUSSOLINI

I did. And to air my shirt. And do my teeth. And wash behind my ears.

That Mussolini should have been a target as early as 1931, when Thomas was only seventeen and Fascism not yet even a fashionable fear, shows a very early 'political' reflex within the comedy.

Under Milk Wood rests on an innocent voyeurism. The idea of visiting the inhabitants of a sleeping community and keeping their dreams as background to their waking day, and forgiving all, drew on techniques already exercised in Thomas's short stories in the early 1930s. These tales are darker-toned than the play, and their characters have more disaffection than affection in them; but the technique remains the same. For example, in 1936 in 'The Orchards' (where significantly Thomas first used the reversible name Llarreggub), 'the day was a passing of days', and Marlais (Thomas's own middle name) is 'a man on the roof', able to view the town while being 'invisible to the street'. We read that 'poor Marlais's morning, turning to evening, spins before you', that 'Marlais's death in life in the circular going down of the day that had taken no time blows again in the wind for you', that 'a baby cried, but the cry grew fainter. It is all one, the loud voice and the still voice striking a common silence, the dowdy lady flattening her nose against the panes, and the well-mourned lady.' The no-chance woman flattening her nose against the window-panes is the Beatles' Eleanor Rigby of the 1930s.

But she is miles away from Bessie Bighead in the play:

Alone until she dies, Bessie Bighead, hired help, born in the workhouse, smelling of the cowshed, snores bass and gruff on a couch of straw in a loft in Salt Lake Farm and picks a posy of daisies in Sunday Meadow to put on the grave of Gomer Owen who kissed her once by the pig-sty when she wasn't looking and never kissed her again although she was looking all the time.

Even the manic Butcher Beynon, teasing his wife that she is eating cat's meat and that he is now 'going out after the corgis, with my little cleaver', is at a great distance from this picture from the short story 'The Horse's Ha' of 1936:

> Butcher and baker fell asleep that night, their women sleeping at their sides . . . Over the shops, the cold eggs that had life, the box where the rats worked all night on the high meat, the shopkeepers gave no thought of death.

In *Under Milk Wood* we have moved from disaffection to affection. Indeed, this darker early material was already moving towards a comic vision long before the writing of the play. In the *Portrait* story 'Just Like Little Dogs' (1939), for example, the narrative and atmosphere, the lyrical embrace, of *Under Milk Wood* were already there:

> I was a lonely nightwalker and a steady stander-at-corners. I liked to walk through the wet town after midnight, when the streets were deserted and the window lights out, alone under the moon, gigantically sad in the damp streets by ghostly Ebenezer Chapel. And I never felt more a part of the remote and overpressing world, or more full of love and arrogance and pity and humility, not for myself alone, but for the living earth I suffered on.

It is clear that the young Dylan Thomas had long been, like Robert Frost, 'one acquainted with the night . . ./ When far away an interrupted cry/ Came over houses from another street.'

But the narration of *Under Milk Wood* is essentially impersonal. The narration is split into two Voices to share the load for the actors delivering them, but it remains in essence the same neutral narration. The two Voices are not themselves characters, but masters of ceremony for 'characters'. They reveal the lives of others, but not through any interaction with those lives. Andrew Sinclair ran up against this simple but crucial fact when he turned the play into a feature film in 1971 (with Richard Burton as First Narrator, as in the original broadcast in 1954). In moving a 'play for voices' onto the big screen, Sinclair was forced to give character and motive to the two narrators – 'Why do they ride into town?' he asked. 'Who are they looking for? . . . What is their power of conjuring up dreams and the dead?' But in the play these are motives the two Voices don't need, and questions that listeners never feel prompted to ask.

'Closer now,' 'Closer still,' 'Coming closer to him' – impersonal techniques learnt from the large number of broadcasts and filmscripts that Thomas wrote in the 1940s helped make real what in the early stories had been mere assertion – that the life of these characters 'spins before you' and 'blows again in the wind for you'. This scene-setting power was now realized more fully in a technology beyond the page. Success depended on talented contact with large audiences, in the cinema or at the wireless-set. The medium belonged to the people because they could be wooed only by talents suited to that medium. Thomas was an intelligent actor, and took part in several plays on radio (as Satan, for example, in a dramatization of Milton's *Paradise Lost*, replacing no less an actor than Paul Scofield), in powerful readings of poetry and prose, and in writing and reading vivid radio essays like 'Holiday Memory' (1946). In fact it was in a review of 'Holiday Memory' in the *New Statesman* that Edward Sackville-West wondered 'why this remarkable poet has never attempted a poetic drama for broadcasting: he would seem to have all the qualities needed'. The poet's wife Caitlin often lamented the scale of this commitment to broadcasting, fearing that it took the poet away from poetry. But it was an honourable means of livelihood in financially desperate times, and there was nothing 'hack' about it. Radio and film were 'applied' challenges to Thomas's verbal talents on the page. And of course the broadcasts themselves slowly matured until, in 'Return Journey' (1947) and *Under Milk Wood*, a division between script and literature is meaningless. Indeed, one of the tragedies is that, by the time *Under Milk Wood* showed a way forward for radio drama after its verbally thin and propagandist duties during the war, radio itself was overtaken by television, a very different medium.

With hindsight, many of the broadcasts and filmscripts seem like trial runs for the play, and 'Quite Early One Morning' (1944) was close to being just that, with a narrator bringing to life the sleeping inhabitants of a small seaside village (New Quay). But in wartime there was neither the luxury nor the confidence for mere trial runs. Quite apart therefore from the technical lessons learnt, there was another, equally important role that the broadcasts and filmscripts played. They kept current moral concerns that in the poems had to be indirect. Thus in 'The Londoner' (broadcast 1946), covering twenty-four hours in the life of an ordinary post-war London family, and opening and closing with night and dreams, one of the main characters says: 'If a bomb had your name on it, you had it coming and that's all. Atom-bombs got everyruddybody's name on 'em, that's the difference.' It's a devastating version of the cliché about the bullet that has your name on it. In the same way, 'The Londoner' and its immediate successor 'Margate – Past and Present' (also 1946) satirized the 'Voice of an Expert' and 'Voice of an Information Book', the voices of cold control-freaks who kill communities, and, given the chance, kill races and nations and the imagination, too. *Under Milk Wood* distils this bloodless quality-control into the quainter, but still uncomprehending, Voice of a Guide-book. The satire can now afford to be paler because the sane good humour fleshed out in this 'place of love' obviously doesn't *need* defending.

But it hadn't always been so. From as early as 1943 Thomas had conceived of the play under the title 'The Town That Was Mad', in which Llareggub is certified insane by an Inspector sent down from London. This was still the intended plot as late as December 1950. A trial is arranged, at which the 'Prosecution' sums up by describing its notion of an ideally 'sane' town. The leading characters – Captain Cat, Eli Jenkins, Organ Morgan and Mr Pugh – decide that if *that* is what sanity looks like, then they would rather be thought mad, and accept isolation from an obviously insane world. Obviously, the plot was pure farce. But the difficulty was that it was a plot at all. Thomas's talents just did not lie in structures of that kind. There was a danger that the work, already long protracted, would never get finished. He was released to write what we now have when his producer at the BBC, Douglas Cleverdon, stressed the difference between a radio play and a radio 'feature':

A radio play is a dramatic work deriving from the tradition of the theatre, but conceived in terms of radio. A radio feature is, roughly, any constructed programme (that is, other than news bulletins, racing commentaries, and so forth) that derives from the technical apparatus of radio ... It has no rules determining what can or cannot be done. And though it may be in dramatic form, it has no need of a dramatic plot.

A 'radio feature' brought into play Thomas's most natural talents.

In any case, though *Under Milk Wood* took years to find its appropriate form, that form had been slowly shaped by all those other broadcasts and films. These were written at an amazingly efficient speed, though never without concentration and research. (In 'Return Journey' Thomas retrieved the exact names of the Swansea shops and businesses destroyed by the German bombs through consulting the Swansea Borough records.) But in one sense the play, too, was written quickly. For one thing there is the speed with which places Thomas lived in became places he wrote about. Caitlin said that in the bar of Brown's Hotel at Laugharne 'he picked up all the character vignettes which he moulded into *Under Milk Wood* ... Dylan captured all that, and the lives of the more respectable people behind their blinds who wouldn't come to the pub anyway, who wore their best Sunday suits, and walked to church with a Bible under their arms: he saw it all.' (With a tragic appropriateness, it was during a broadcast, from Laugharne itself, of part of his recorded script 'Laugharne' that the cable announcing Thomas's final collapse in New York was handed to his wife in the audience.) In the same way, writing the play and writing about it seemed quickly suffused with the same language. Thomas's letter to the editor of *Botteghe Oscure*, the Rome-based magazine where a version of the first half was published in April 1952, said that the work would develop 'through the multifariously busy little town evening of meals and drinks and loves and quarrels and dreams and wishes, into the night' – a sentence that has the very cadence of the play itself. And though not about *Under Milk Wood* at all, the 1949 broadcast 'Living in Wales' was already full of the very words that swarm and hum through the play: words like *bellying, dredger, gloved, laver-bread, bombazine, minto-sucking, bootlaces, china dogs* and *brilliantine*.

Though the physical writing was protracted, the imaginative ingredients were spontaneous, not just hammered out. It was all the more important therefore that they should also be carefully sifted and filtered. Innumerable character sketches, descriptions, ideas, sentences and phrases remain unused in the manuscripts now at the University of Texas, along with hints of material that Thomas would have liked to add to the evening section at the end, to give a greater sense of 'balance' to the whole. But also among the manuscripts are notes for such things as 'the tragedy behind Lord Cut Glass's life' or 'Mrs Ogmore-Pritchard's terrible death-waiting loneliness'. They show that Thomas could at any stage have written a darker play. But the background of the world situation was already dark enough, and it was a comic opening of doors and windows that won the day. But we can still only marvel at the play's unity of tone across such a wide range of forms – narration, description, commentary, dialogue, monologue, song, poem, ballad, children's games, cockcrows and mere noises. Every detail serves lyrically or satirically the need for simple generosity of spirit. Even Mrs Ogmore-Pritchard 'cannot drive out the Spring: from one of her fingerbowls, a primrose grows'. It is a masterly touch, as efficient as the Lady's frigid unawareness that she is twisting a stalk from her bowl of lilacs in T. S. Eliot's 'Portrait of a Lady', just as the 'atmosphere of Juliet's tomb' in the same Eliot poem comes to mind when we hear that 'an icicle forms in the cold air of the dining vault' when Mr and Mrs Pugh are eating. At different ends of the tragic-comic spectrum real poets are at work.

Though deeply Welsh, there was always something refreshingly shareable about the play, even internationally. New York in 1953 provided its first audience, and understood it all. America has always been good at portraits of small communities – Edgar Lee Masters's *Spoon River Anthology*, for example, in which the dead of a small Midwest town deliver brief messages from beyond the grave, and on which Thomas in 1952 wrote an excellent radio script which unfortunately he did not live to record. All Thomas had to do with *Under Milk Wood* for an American audience was to change, pro tem, *parchs* to preachers, *gippo's* to gypsies', *sago* to dumplings, *doctored* to neutered, *workhouse* to poorhouse. He insisted, though, that even the American Polly Garter should say *loving* not *lovin'*. It was a nice touch, because the only other thing he asked of those five brave American actors who joined him in the first readings in New York City in 1953 was that they should 'love the words . . . *Love* the words'.

Table of Dates

three years Thomas acts in many productions at the Swansea
Little Theatre – e.g. as Simon Bliss in Coward's *Hay Fever*,
Count Bellair in Farquhar's *The Beaux' Stratagem*, and the Host in
The Merry Wives of Windsor.

1932   *16 December* Leaves his full-time post with the *South Wales Daily
Post*, but continues with freelance journalism, concentrating also
on getting his poems published in London. The first of many
visits to London in search of a job.

1933   *March* 'And death shall have no dominion' published in the *New
English Weekly*, Thomas's first London publication.
7 June Listed as one of twenty-eight winners out of 11,000
contestants in a BBC poetry competition: the poem was read
on the BBC National Service, 28 June.
August Visits London (his married sister lives in a houseboat on
the Thames) to place poems with periodicals, notably the *New
English Weekly* and the *Adelphi*.
September 'That Sanity Be Kept', the first of many poems
published in the 'Poet's Corner' of Victor Neuberg's *Sunday
Referee*. Starts correspondence with Pamela Hansford Johnson.
10 September Thomas's father admitted to University College
Hospital, London, for successful treatment for cancer of the
throat.
November From now on, Thomas is also writing short stories,
and reviewing for London periodicals.

1934   *14 March* The publication of 'Light breaks where no sun shines'
in the *Listener* prompts inquiries from Stephen Spender and
Geoffrey Grigson. Another poet to encourage him at this stage
is T. S. Eliot, who later regrets not booking him for Faber.
22 April 'The force that through the green fuse' wins the 'book
prize' of the *Sunday Referee* – the sponsorship of his first volume
of poems. Much journeying for the next few years between
Swansea and London.
20–22 May First stay at Laugharne (a Whitsun weekend in the
company of Glyn Jones).
20–21 October Visits (with Glyn Jones) Caradoc Evans at
Aberystwyth.

11 November Moves to London to share rooms with Swansea artist friends, Fred Janes and Mervyn Levy.

18 December 18 Poems (his first volume of poetry) published by the *Sunday Referee* and the Parton Bookshop.

1935 *March* First meeting (back in Swansea) with Vernon Watkins, immediate friend and major correspondent.

July–August At Glen Lough, County Donegal (with Geoffrey Grigson).

1936 *8 April* To Cornwall (Penzance and Mousehole) until 20 May. First meeting with his future wife, Caitlin Macnamara.

11 June Attends the opening of the International Surrealist Exhibition at the New Burlington Galleries in London.

10 September Twenty-five Poems published by Dent.

18 December The poet's father's last day at the Grammar School.

1937 W. H. Auden and Michael Roberts choose 'We lying by seasand' for a special 'English Number' of *Poetry* (Chicago), Thomas's first publication in America.

March His parents move to Bishopston, outside Swansea.

21 April Thomas's first broadcast, 'Life and the Modern Poet', starts a long career in broadcasting.

11 July Marries Caitlin Macnamara at the Register Office in Penzance.

1 September Leaves Cornwall to stay at his parents' new home outside Swansea.

1 October Moves to his mother-in-law's house at Blashford in Hampshire.

1938 *January* Writes to Henry Treece, supporting the book Treece is planning on his poetry.

March First negotiations (with James Laughlin) for American publication of his work.

April Moves from Blashford to his parents' house outside Swansea, and then *(May)* to Laugharne. With London, these would be his main homes for the next three years.

November Poetry (Chicago) awards him its Oscar Blumenthal Prize.

1939　*30 January* First child, Llewelyn, born in the hospital at Poole, Dorset.

24 August The Map of Love (poetry and prose) published by Dent.

3 September Second World War declared.

20 December The World I Breathe, a selection of Thomas's poetry and prose, published by New Directions in New York – his first volume publication in America.

1940　*4 April Portrait of the Artist as a Young Dog* (autobiographical short stories) published by Dent

6 April Registers for military service, but later turned down on medical grounds.

4 July Moves with other artists to John Davenport's house at Marshfield in Gloucestershire. Until November, collaborates with Davenport on a parodic novel, *The Death of the King's Canary*.

24 September American edition of *Portrait of the Artist as a Young Dog* published.

1941　*22–24 February* Incendiary bombs devastate Swansea.

April Decides to sell the poetry notebooks and other material. The last poem taken from the notebooks for publication is 'The Hunchback in the Park'.

October Starts as script-writer for Strand Films.

1942　*20 August* Joins Caitlin in Talsarn, Cardiganshire. The start of a period in different parts of West Wales that in 1944–5 saw a burst of new writing in the otherwise lean years of the war.

1943　*7 January* Records 'Reminiscences of Childhood' for BBC Welsh Home Service.

25 January New Poems published by New Directions in New York.

3 March Daughter, Aeronwy, born in London. She is named after the Aeron river in Cardiganshire.

September The family joins Thomas's parents at Llangain, near the now famous farm Fernhill (subject of the poem 'Fern Hill').

1944　*February* Family moves to a cottage near Bosham in Sussex to avoid the London bombing raids, but still retains a flat in Chelsea.

June After the closure of Strand Films, Thomas is kept on at Gryphon Films. He later writes also for Stratford Film and Gainsborough Films.

6 June D-Day.

4 September Family moves to New Quay, a small fishing village on Cardigan Bay – along with Laugharne, the main inspiration for the setting of *Under Milk Wood*.

14 December Records in London 'Quite Early One Morning' (a direct precursor of *Under Milk Wood*) for later transmission by the BBC Welsh Home Service.

1945 *8 May* VE Day.

July Leaves New Quay.

15 August VJ Day.

6 December Records 'Memories of Christmas' for the BBC Welsh Service Children's Hour.

1946 From early 1946 to May 1949 living in or near Oxford.

7 February Deaths and Entrances (poems) published by Dent.

24 March Signs, at T. S. Eliot's request, a letter in support of Ezra Pound.

13 May Reads 'Fern Hill', Lawrence's 'Snake' and Blake's 'Tyger' in the Command Performance for the Queen at Wigmore Hall.

8 November Selected Writings published by New Directions in New York.

1947 *10–12 February* Revisits Swansea to collect information for the broadcast 'Return Journey'.

April–August A family visit, via Calais, Switzerland and Milan, to Rapallo, funded by a Society of Authors award on Edith Sitwell's recommendation – her way of saving him from having to go to America.

12 August Settles at South Leigh, near Witney, Oxfordshire.

1948 *February* Thomas at Llangain looking after his father, while his mother is in hospital.

21 April Rents a cottage at South Leigh for his parents, who are both ill.

1949 *4–9 March* Attends an artists' conference in Prague at the invitation of the Czech cultural attaché in London.

May The family moves to the Boat House at Laugharne.

28 May Receives and accepts the first invitation by John Malcolm Brinnin, Director of the Poetry Center in New York City, to visit America on a lecture tour.

24 July Son, Colm, born in Carmarthen Hospital.

6 August Contributes first piece ('Over Sir John's Hill') to Marguerite Caetani's magazine *Botteghe Oscure* in Rome, soon also to receive poems like 'Lament' and 'Do not go gentle into that good night'; and the first published version of a part of *Under Milk Wood*.

1950 *20 February* Flies to New York on his first American tour, returning 31 May on the liner *Queen Elizabeth*, after around forty public readings. This hectic schedule remains the pattern for another three American tours.

1–6 September John Malcolm Brinnin visits Thomas at Laugharne.

1951 *8 January–14 February* In Persia to write a documentary filmscript for the Anglo-Iranian Oil Company.

1952 *15 January* Thomas and Caitlin embark on the *Queen Mary* for a second American tour, returning on the *New Amsterdam* four months later.

February In Country Sleep (poems) published in America only.

9 October Agrees to J. Alexander Rolph's compiling a bibliography of his works.

10 November Collected Poems 1934–1952, published by Dent, sells 30,000 copies in the English edition alone.

16 December Thomas's father dies, aged seventy-six.

1953 *20 January* Receives the William Foyle Poetry Prize for 1952.

31 March American edition of *Collected Poems 1934–1952* published by New Directions in New York.

16 April On the *United States* en route for his third American tour. Death of his sister Nancy.

14 May Under Milk Wood's first performance at the Poetry Center in New York. *The Doctor and the Devils* becomes the first of the filmscripts to be published.

23 May Discusses with Stravinsky in Boston collaboration for an opera.

3 June Flies home, the day after the coronation of Queen Elizabeth II.

5 October Reads part of *Under Milk Wood* at the Tenby Arts Club.

8 October The filmscript *The Doctor and the Devils* published by New Directions in New York.

9 October Leaves Laugharne en route, via Swansea, for his flight on 19 October for his final American tour. Delivers *Under Milk Wood* to the BBC for typing.

20 October– Though ill, Thomas commits himself in rehearsals of *Under Milk Wood* to performances at the Poetry Center in New York on the 24th and 25th, and to a symposium at City College, New York, on 'Film Art' (in a group including Arthur Miller) on the 28th.

27 October Thomas's thirty-ninth birthday.

4 November Ill and in pain, Thomas is injected with an overdose of morphine by a New York doctor. Falls into a coma.

7 November Caitlin Thomas flies to New York.

9 November Thomas dies at St Vincent's Hospital, New York City.

24 November Buried at St Martin's Church in Laugharne.

1982 *1 March* Memorial stone laid in Poets' Corner, Westminster Abbey.

Further Reading

EDITIONS

Thomas, Dylan, *Collected Stories*, ed. Walford Davies, introduced by
    Leslie Norris, Dent, 1983.
— *Collected Poems 1934–1953*, ed. Walford Davies and Ralph Maud,
    Dent, 1988.
— *The Notebook Poems*, ed. Ralph Maud, Dent, 1989.
— *The Broadcasts*, ed. Ralph Maud, Dent, 1991.
— *Selected Poems*, ed. Walford Davies, Dent, 1993.
— *The Filmscripts*, ed. John Ackerman, Dent, 1995.
— *The Dylan Thomas Omnibus*, Dent, 1995. Incorporating *Under Milk
    Wood* with Thomas's poems, stories and broadcasts.
— *Under Milk Wood: A Play for Voices*, ed. Walford Davies and Ralph
    Maud, Dent, 1995.

TEXT

Cleverdon, Douglas, *The Growth of Milk Wood*, Dent, 1969.

RECORDINGS

Dylan Thomas Reading his Complete Recorded Poetry, Caedmon Publishers,
    LP recording TC 2014, New York, 1963.
Under Milk Wood. Caedmon Publishers, LP recording TC 2005, New
    York, 1954. A recording of the first completed text in a stage
    reading at the Poetry Center of New York's Young Men's and

Young Women's Hebrew Association, 14 May 1953. Directed by Dylan Thomas, who participated as First Voice and as the Reverend Eli Jenkins.

Under Milk Wood. Argo Record Company, LP recording RG 21, London, 1954. A recording of the first BBC production, Third Programme, 25 January 1954. Produced by Douglas Cleverdon, with Richard Burton as First Voice.

BIOGRAPHY

Brinnin, John Malcolm, *Dylan Thomas in America*, Dent, 1956.

Ferris, Paul, *Caitlin: The Life of Caitlin Thomas*, Hutchinson, 1993.

— *Dylan Thomas: The Biography*, new edition, Dent, 1999. The standard biography of 1977, revised and updated.

FitzGibbon, Constantine, *The Life of Dylan Thomas*, Dent, 1965.

Jones, Daniel, *My Friend Dylan Thomas*, Dent, 1977.

Sinclair, Andrew, *Dylan Thomas: Poet of His People*, Michael Joseph, 1975.

Thomas, Caitlin, with George Tremlett, *Caitlin: A Warring Absence*, Secker & Warburg, 1986.

Watkins, Gwen, *Portrait of a Friend*, Gomer, 1983.

LETTERS

Dylan Thomas: *Collected Letters*, ed. Paul Ferris, Dent, 2000. The authoritative *Collected Letters* of 1985, enlarged and updated.

BIBLIOGRAPHY

Gaston, Georg M. A., *Dylan Thomas: A Reference Guide*, G. K. Hall, 1987.

Harris, John, *A Bibliographical Guide to Twenty-four Modern Anglo-Welsh Writers*, University of Wales Press, 1994.

— Updating bibliographies of Anglo-Welsh writers, including Dylan Thomas, in *Welsh Writing in English: A Yearbook of Critical Essays*, ed. Tony Brown, *New Welsh Review*, 1995 onwards.

Maud, Ralph, *Dylan Thomas in Print: A Bibliographical History* (with an
appendix by Walford Davies), Dent, 1970.
Rolph, J. Alexander, *Dylan Thomas: A Bibliography*, Dent, 1956.

CRITICAL AND OTHER STUDIES

Ackerman, John, *Dylan Thomas: His Life and Work*, Macmillan, 1991.
— *Welsh Dylan*, Seven, 1998.
— *A Dylan Thomas Companion: Life, Poetry and Prose*, Macmillan, 1991.
Bayley, John, *The Romantic Survival*, Constable, 1957.
Davies, James A., *Dylan Thomas's Places: A Biographical and Literary
Guide*, Christopher Davies, 1987.
— *A Reference Companion to Dylan Thomas*, Greenwood Press, 1998.
Davies, Walford, *Dylan Thomas*, University of Wales Press, 1990.
— *Dylan Thomas*, Open University Press, 1986.
— *Dylan Thomas: The Poet in His Chains*, the W. D. Thomas Memorial
Lecture, the University of Wales, Swansea, 1986.
Holbrook, David, 'Two Welsh Writers: T. F. Powys and Dylan
Thomas', *Pelican Guide to English Literature: The Modern Age*,
ed. Boris Ford, Penguin Books, 1961.
— *Llareggub Revisited: Dylan Thomas and the State of Modern Poetry*, Bowes
& Bowes, 1962.
Lerner, Laurence, 'Sex in Arcadia', in *Dylan Thomas: New Critical Essays*,
ed. Walford Davies, Dent, 1972.
Lewis, Peter, 'Return Journey to Milk Wood', *Poetry Wales* 9, 1973.
— '*Under Milk Wood* as Radio Poem', *Anglo-Welsh Review* 64, 1979.
— 'The Radio Road to Llareggub', in *British Radio Drama*, ed. John
Drakakis, Cambridge University Press, 1981.
Mathias, Roland, 'Any Minute or Dark Day Now: The Writing of
Under Milk Wood', in his *A Ride through the Wood: Essays on
Anglo-Welsh Literature*, Poetry Wales Press, 1985.
Maud, Ralph, *Entrances to Dylan Thomas' Poetry*, University of
Pittsburgh Press, 1963.
Mayer, Ann Elizabeth, *Artists in Dylan Thomas's Prose Works*, McGill–
Queen's University Press, 1995.
Peach, Linden, *The Prose Writing of Dylan Thomas*, Macmillan, 1988.

Watson, Daphne B., 'Voices Still Singing: A Revaluation of *Under Milk Wood*', in *Dylan Thomas: Craft or Sullen Art*, ed. Alan Bold, Vision Press, 1990.

Williams, Raymond, 'Dylan Thomas's Play for Voices', *Critical Quarterly* I, Spring 1959.

A Note on the Text

The text for the present edition is based on that of *Dylan Thomas: Under Milk Wood, A Play for Voices*, edited by Walford Davies and Ralph Maud, Dent, 1995 – but with the changes and variations described in the last paragraph below. The 1995 Davies–Maud text superseded that of the previous standard Dent edition by Daniel Jones (1954), in the main by correcting all readings in the latter that had no manuscript authority. In addition to various other provisional forms of the play, the Davies–Maud edition paid strict attention to the two manuscripts that received Dylan Thomas's latest attention in 1953, the last year of his life. Those two manuscripts can be described as follows.

1. The first derived from that typed for the play's première in New York on 14 May 1953. Back in Laugharne, Thomas wrote out (with some changes and some minor errors) twenty-three foolscap pages of a fair copy corresponding to the first nineteen pages of the New York typescript, and then attached pages 20 to 51 of the typescript to the fair copy. En route again for America in October 1953, he gave this composite text to the BBC in London to type onto duplicating stencils in the BBC script format. He collected the original, and then lost it, but told Douglas Cleverdon, the commissioning BBC producer, that if he found it, it was his to keep. Cleverdon found it in a Soho pub. The Trustees of the Dylan Thomas Estate challenged legal ownership, but lost. Cleverdon later sold it privately. After 1969, the manuscript was lost from public view. In 1994 it was traced by Walford Davies and Ralph Maud to the Rosenbach Museum and Library, Philadelphia.

2. The second manuscript is the typescript prepared by the BBC and given to Thomas on his loss of the above original. This became the poet's working copy during the performances of 24 and 25 October

1953 in New York, during the last two weeks of his life. It was deposited at the Beinecke Rare Book and Manuscript Library, Yale University, in 1961. It contains all the corrections, revisions and deletions made by Thomas just before his death. But these were made in the hectic conditions of haste and illness.

The 1995 Davies–Maud edition therefore chose to reconcile the best intentions and instincts of (1) and (2) above. In terms of the actual wording of the whole play, the 1995 Dent version is as definitive as it is possible to be where a text of long gestation, and at the end written against time and illness, has to be posthumously adjudicated by editors.

But the Davies–Maud edition was designed specifically as a 'reading' edition. To that end, it chose to merge the First Voice and Second Voice into one italicized narration, and also to omit the names of characters at certain points where their words have been only momentarily interrupted by another voice or by a stage direction. In the present edition, the First and Second Voice attributions are restored, along with every character's name, however briefly interrupted. I have also returned the narrating voices to roman type, but have kept their wider line-length so as to differentiate the narration from the narrower gauge of the speech of the characters themselves. I have returned stage directions to italic and made several minor silent corrections – for example, in alineation – when validated by the two manuscript sources described above.

Under Milk Wood

[*Silence*]

FIRST VOICE [*Very softly*] To begin at the beginning:

It is spring, moonless night in the small town, starless and bible-black, the cobblestreets silent and the hunched, courters'-and-rabbits' wood limping invisible down to the sloeblack, slow, black, crowblack, fishingboat-bobbing sea. The houses are blind as moles (though moles see fine tonight in the snouting, velvet dingles) or blind as Captain Cat there in the muffled middle by the pump and the town clock, the shops in mourning, the Welfare Hall in widows' weeds. And all the people of the lulled and dumbfound town are sleeping now.

Hush, the babies are sleeping, the farmers, the fishers, the tradesmen and pensioners, cobbler, schoolteacher, postman and publican, the undertaker and the fancy woman, drunkard, dressmaker, preacher, policeman, the webfoot cocklewomen and the tidy wives. Young girls lie bedded soft or glide in their dreams, with rings and trousseaux, bridesmaided by glow-worms down the aisles of the organplaying wood. The boys are dreaming wicked or of the bucking ranches of the night and the jolly, rodgered sea. And the anthracite statues of the horses sleep in the fields, and the cows in the byres, and the dogs in the wetnosed yards; and the cats nap in the slant corners or lope sly, streaking and needling, on the one cloud of the roofs.

You can hear the dew falling, and the hushed town breathing.

Only your eyes are unclosed, to see the black and folded town fast, and slow, asleep.

And you alone can hear the invisible starfall, the darkest-before-dawn minutely dewgrazed stir of the black, dab-filled sea where the Arethusa, the Curlew and the Skylark, Zanzibar, Rhiannon, the Rover, the Cormorant, and the Star of Wales tilt and ride.

Listen. It is night moving in the streets, the processional salt slow musical wind in Coronation Street and Cockle Row, it is the grass growing on Llareggub Hill, dewfall, starfall, the sleep of birds in Milk Wood.

Listen. It is night in the chill, squat chapel, hymning, in bonnet and brooch and bombazine black, butterfly choker and bootlace bow, coughing like nannygoats, sucking mintoes, fortywinking hallelujah; night in the four-ale, quiet as a domino; in Ocky Milkman's loft like a mouse with gloves; in Dai Bread's bakery flying like black flour. It is tonight in Donkey Street, trotting silent, with seaweed on its hooves, along the cockled cobbles, past curtained fernpot, text and trinket, harmonium, holy dresser, watercolours done by hand, china dog and rosy tin teacaddy. It is night neddying among the snuggeries of babies.

Look. It is night, dumbly, royally winding through the Coronation cherry trees; going through the graveyard of Bethesda with winds gloved and folded, and dew doffed; tumbling by the Sailors' Arms.

Time passes. Listen. Time passes.

Come closer now.

Only you can hear the houses sleeping in the streets in the slow deep salt and silent black, bandaged night. Only you can see, in the blinded bedrooms, the coms and petticoats over the chairs, the jugs and basins, the glasses of teeth, Thou Shalt Not on the wall, and the yellowing dickybird-watching pictures of the dead. Only you can hear and see, behind the eyes of the sleepers, the movements and countries and mazes and colours and dismays and rainbows and tunes and wishes and flight and fall and despairs and big seas of their dreams.

From where you are, you can hear their dreams.

Captain Cat, the retired blind seacaptain, asleep in his bunk in the seashelled, ship-in-bottled, shipshape best cabin of Schooner House dreams of

SECOND VOICE never such seas as any that swamped the decks of his S.S. Kidwelly bellying over the bedclothes and jellyfish-slippery sucking him down salt deep into the Davy dark where the fish come biting out and nibble him down to his wishbone and the long drowned nuzzle up to him . . .

FIRST DROWNED

Remember me, Captain?

CAPTAIN CAT

You're Dancing Williams!

FIRST DROWNED

I lost my step in Nantucket.

SECOND DROWNED

Do you see me, Captain? the white bone talking? I'm Tom-Fred the donkeyman . . . We shared the same girl once . . . Her name was Mrs Probert . . .

WOMAN'S VOICE

Rosie Probert, thirty three Duck Lane. Come on up, boys, I'm dead.

THIRD DROWNED

Hold me, Captain, I'm Jonah Jarvis, come to a bad end, very enjoyable . . .

FOURTH DROWNED

Alfred Pomeroy Jones, sealawyer, born in Mumbles, sung like a linnet, crowned with you a flagon, tattooed with mermaids, thirst like a dredger, died of blisters . . .

FIRST DROWNED

This skull at your earhole is

FIFTH DROWNED

Curly Bevan. Tell my auntie it was me that pawned the ormolu clock . . .

CAPTAIN CAT

Aye, aye, Curly.

SECOND DROWNED

Tell my missus no my never

THIRD DROWNED

I never done what she said I never . . .

FOURTH DROWNED

Yes, they did.

FIFTH DROWNED

And who brings cocoanuts and shawls and parrots to *my* Gwen now?

FIRST DROWNED
How's it above?

SECOND DROWNED
Is there rum and lavabread?

THIRD DROWNED
Bosoms and robins?

FOURTH DROWNED
Concertinas?

FIFTH DROWNED
Ebenezer's bell?

FIRST DROWNED
Fighting and onions?

SECOND DROWNED
And sparrows and daisies?

THIRD DROWNED
Tiddlers in a jamjar?

FOURTH DROWNED
Buttermilk and whippets?

FIFTH DROWNED
Rock-a-bye baby?

FIRST DROWNED
Washing on the line?

SECOND DROWNED
And old girls in the snug?

THIRD DROWNED
How's the tenors in Dowlais?

FOURTH DROWNED
Who milks the cows in Maesgwyn?

FIFTH DROWNED
When she smiles, is there dimples?

FIRST DROWNED
What's the smell of parsley?

CAPTAIN CAT
Oh, my dead dears!

FIRST VOICE From where you are, you can hear, in Cockle Row in the spring, moonless, night, Miss Price, dressmaker and sweetshop-keeper dream of

SECOND VOICE her lover, tall as the town clock tower, Samson-syrup-gold-maned, whacking thighed and piping hot, thunderbolt-bass'd and barnacle-breasted flailing up the cockles with his eyes like blowlamps and scooping low over her lonely loving hotwaterbottled body . . .

MR EDWARDS

    Myfanwy Price!

MISS PRICE

    Mr Mog Edwards!

MR EDWARDS

    I am a draper mad with love. I love you more than all the flannelette and calico, candlewick, dimity, crash and merino, tussore, cretonne, crepon, muslin, poplin, ticking and twill in the whole Cloth Hall of the world. I have come to take you away to my Emporium on the hill, where the change hums on wires. Throw away your little bedsocks and your Welsh wool knitted jacket, I will warm the sheets like an electric toaster, I will lie by your side like the Sunday roast . . .

MISS PRICE

    I will knit you a wallet of forget-me-not blue, for the money to be comfy. I will warm your heart by the fire so that you can slip it in under your vest when the shop is closed . . .

MR EDWARDS

    Myfanwy, Myfanwy, before the mice gnaw at your bottom drawer will you say

MISS PRICE

    Yes, Mog, yes, Mog, yes, yes, yes . . .

MR EDWARDS

    And all the bells of the tills of the town shall ring for our wedding.

    [*Noise of money-tills and chapel bells.*]

FIRST VOICE Come now, drift up the dark, come up the drifting sea-dark street now in the dark night seesawing like the sea, to the bible-black airless attic over Jack Black the cobbler's shop where alone and savagely Jack Black sleeps in a nightshirt tied to his ankles with elastic and dreams of

SECOND VOICE chasing the naughty couples down the grassgreen gooseberried double bed of the wood, flogging the tosspots in the spit-and-sawdust, driving out the bare, bold girls from the sixpenny hops of his nightmares ...

JACK BLACK [*Loudly*]
    Ach y fi!
    Ach y fi!

FIRST VOICE Evans the Death, the undertaker,

EVANS THE DEATH
    laughs high and aloud in his sleep and curls up his toes as he sees, upon waking fifty years ago, snow lie deep on the goosefield behind the sleeping house; and he runs out into the field where his mother is making Welshcakes in the snow, and steals a fistfull of snowflakes and currants and climbs back to bed to eat them cold and sweet under the warm, white clothes while his mother dances in the snow kitchen crying out for her lost currants.

FIRST VOICE And in the little pink-eyed cottage next to the undertaker's, lie, alone, the seventeen snoring gentle stone of Mister Waldo, rabbitcatcher, barber, herbalist, catdoctor, quack, his fat, pink hands, palms up, over the edge of the patchwork quilt, his black boots neat and tidy in the washing basin, his bowler on a nail above the bed, a milk stout and a slice of cold bread pudding under the pillow; and, dripping in the dark, he dreams of

MOTHER
    This little piggy went to market
    This little piggy stayed at home
    This little piggy had roast beef

This little piggy had none
And this little piggy went

LITTLE BOY

wee wee wee wee wee

MOTHER

all the way home to

WIFE [*Screaming*]

Waldo! Wal-do!

MR WALDO

Yes, Blodwen love?

WIFE

Oh, what'll the neighbours say, what'll the neighbours . . .

FIRST NEIGHBOUR

Poor Mrs Waldo

SECOND NEIGHBOUR

What she puts up with

FIRST NEIGHBOUR

Never should of married

SECOND NEIGHBOUR

If she didn't had to

FIRST NEIGHBOUR

Same as her mother.

SECOND NEIGHBOUR

There's a husband for you

FIRST NEIGHBOUR

Bad as his father

SECOND NEIGHBOUR

And you know where he ended

FIRST NEIGHBOUR

Up in the asylum

SECOND NEIGHBOUR

Crying for his ma.

FIRST NEIGHBOUR

Every Saturday

SECOND NEIGHBOUR

He hasn't got a leg

FIRST NEIGHBOUR
    And carrying on
SECOND NEIGHBOUR
    With that Mrs Beattie Morris
FIRST NEIGHBOUR
    Up in the quarry
SECOND NEIGHBOUR
    And seen her baby
FIRST NEIGHBOUR
    It's got his nose.
SECOND NEIGHBOUR
    Oh, it makes my heart bleed
FIRST NEIGHBOUR
    What he'll do for drink
SECOND NEIGHBOUR
    He sold the pianola
FIRST NEIGHBOUR
    And her sewing machine
SECOND NEIGHBOUR
    Falling in the gutter
FIRST NEIGHBOUR
    Talking to the lamp-post
SECOND NEIGHBOUR
    Using language
FIRST NEIGHBOUR
    Singing in the w.
SECOND NEIGHBOUR
    Poor Mrs Waldo.
WIFE [*Tearfully*]
    Oh, Waldo, Waldo!
MR WALDO
    Hush, love, hush. I'm widower Waldo now.
MOTHER [*Screaming*]
    Waldo, Wal-do!
LITTLE BOY
    Yes, our mum?

MOTHER

Oh, what'll the neighbours say, what'll the neighbours . . .

THIRD NEIGHBOUR

Black as a chimbley

FOURTH NEIGHBOUR

Ringing doorbells

THIRD NEIGHBOUR

Breaking windows

FOURTH NEIGHBOUR

Making mudpies

THIRD NEIGHBOUR

Stealing currants

FOURTH NEIGHBOUR

Chalking words

THIRD NEIGHBOUR

Saw him in the bushes

FOURTH NEIGHBOUR

Playing moochins

THIRD NEIGHBOUR

Send him to bed without any supper

FOURTH NEIGHBOUR

Give him sennapods and lock him in the dark

THIRD NEIGHBOUR

Off to the reformatory

FOURTH NEIGHBOUR

Off to the reformatory

TOGETHER

Learn him with a slipper on his b.t.m.

ANOTHER MOTHER [*Screaming*]

Waldo, Wal-do! what you doing with our Matti?

LITTLE BOY

Give us a kiss, Matti Richards.

LITTLE GIRL

Give us a penny then.

MR WALDO

I only got a halfpenny.

FIRST WOMAN
> Lips is a penny.

PREACHER
> Will you take this woman Matti Richards

SECOND WOMAN
> Dulcie Prothero

THIRD WOMAN
> Effie Bevan

FOURTH WOMAN
> Lil the Gluepot

FIFTH WOMAN
> Mrs Flusher

WIFE
> Blodwen Bowen

PREACHER
> to be your awful wedded wife

LITTLE BOY [*Screaming*]
> No, no, no!

FIRST VOICE Now, in her iceberg-white, holily laundered crinoline nightgown, under virtuous polar sheets, in her spruced and scoured dust-defying bedroom in trig and trim Bay View, a house for paying guests, at the top of the town, Mrs Ogmore-Pritchard, widow, twice, of Mr Ogmore, linoleum, retired, and Mr Pritchard, failed bookmaker, who, maddened by besoming, swabbing and scrubbing, the voice of the vacuum-cleaner and the fume of polish, ironically swallowed disinfectant, fidgets in her rinsed sleep, wakes in a dream, and nudges in the ribs dead Mr Ogmore, dead Mr Pritchard, ghostly on either side.

MRS OGMORE-PRITCHARD
> Mr Ogmore!
> Mr Pritchard!
> It is time to inhale your balsam.

MR OGMORE
> Oh, Mrs Ogmore!

MR PRITCHARD
> Oh, Mrs Pritchard!

MRS OGMORE-PRITCHARD

> Soon it will be time to get up.
>
> Tell me your tasks, in order.

MR OGMORE

> I must put my pyjamas in the drawer marked pyjamas.

MR PRITCHARD

> I must take my cold bath which is good for me.

MR OGMORE

> I must wear my flannel band to ward off sciatica.

MR PRITCHARD

> I must dress behind the curtain and put on my apron.

MR OGMORE

> I must blow my nose.

MRS OGMORE-PRITCHARD

> in the garden, if you please.

MR OGMORE

> in a piece of tissue-paper which I afterwards burn.

MR PRITCHARD

> I must take my salts which are nature's friend.

MR OGMORE

> I must boil the drinking water because of germs.

MR PRITCHARD

> I must make my herb tea which is free from tannin

MR OGMORE

> and have a charcoal biscuit which is good for me.

MR PRITCHARD

> I may smoke one pipe of asthma mixture

MRS OGMORE-PRITCHARD

> in the woodshed, if you please.

MR PRITCHARD

> and dust the parlour and spray the canary.

MR OGMORE

> I must put on rubber gloves and search the peke for fleas.

MR PRITCHARD

> I must dust the blinds and then I must raise them.

MRS OGMORE-PRITCHARD
　　And before you let the sun in, mind it wipes its shoes.

FIRST VOICE In Butcher Beynon's, Gossamer Beynon, daughter, schoolteacher, dreaming deep, daintily ferrets under a fluttering hummock of chicken's feathers in a slaughterhouse that has chintz curtains and a three-piece suite, and finds, with no surprise, a small rough ready man with a bushy tail winking in a paper carrier.

ORGAN MORGAN
　　Help,

FIRST VOICE cries Organ Morgan, the organist, in his dream,

ORGAN MORGAN
　　　　there is perturbation and music in Coronation Street! All
　　the spouses are honking like geese and the babies singing opera.
　　P.C. Atilla Rees has got his truncheon out and is playing
　　cadenzas by the pump, the cows from Sunday Meadow ring like
　　reindeer, and on the roof of Handel Villa see the Women's
　　Welfare hoofing, bloomered, in the moon.
GOSSAMER BEYNON
　　At last, my love,

SECOND VOICE sighs Gossamer Beynon. And the bushy tail wags rude and ginger.

FIRST VOICE At the sea-end of town, Mr and Mrs Floyd, the cocklers, are sleeping as quiet as death, side by wrinkled side, toothless, salt, and brown, like two old kippers in a box.
　　And high above, in Salt Lake Farm, Mr Utah Watkins counts, all night, the wife-faced sheep as they leap the fences on the hill, smiling and knitting and bleating just like Mrs Utah Watkins.

UTAH WATKINS [*Yawning*]
　　Thirty four, thirty five, thirty six, forty eight,
　　eighty nine . . .
MRS UTAH WATKINS
　　Knit one slip one

Knit two together
Pass the slipstitch over . . .
[*Mrs Utah Watkins bleats.*]

FIRST VOICE Ocky Milkman, drowned asleep in Cockle Street, is emptying his churns into the Dewi River,

OCKY MILKMAN [*Whispering*]
    regardless of expense,

FIRST VOICE and weeping like a funeral.

SECOND VOICE Cherry Owen, next door, lifts a tankard to his lips but nothing flows out of it. He shakes the tankard. It turns into a fish. He drinks the fish.

FIRST VOICE P.C. Atilla Rees

ATILLA REES
    lumps out of bed, dead to the dark, and still foghorning, and
    drags out his helmet from under the bed; but deep in the
    backyard lock-up of his sleep a mean voice murmurs,

A VOICE [*Murmuring*]
    You'll be sorry for this in the morning,
ATILLA REES
    and he heave-ho's back to bed. His helmet swashes in the dark.

SECOND VOICE Willy Nilly, postman, asleep up street, walks fourteen miles to deliver the post as he does every day of the night, and rat-a-tats hard and sharp on Mrs Willy Nilly.

MRS WILLY NILLY
    Don't spank me, please, teacher,

SECOND VOICE whimpers his wife at his side, but every night of her married life she has been late for school.

FIRST VOICE Sinbad Sailors, over the taproom of the Sailors' Arms, hugs his damp pillow whose secret name is Gossamer Beynon.
    A mogul catches Lily Smalls in the wash-house.

LILY SMALLS
Ooh, you old mogul!

SECOND VOICE Mrs Rose-Cottage's eldest, Mae, peels off her pink-and-white skin in a furnace in a tower in a cave in a waterfall in a wood and waits there raw as an onion for Mister Right to leap up the burning tall hollow splashes of leaves like a brilliantined trout.

MAE ROSE-COTTAGE
[*Very close and softly, drawing out the words*]
Call me Dolores
Like they do in the stories.

FIRST VOICE Alone until she dies, Bessie Bighead, hired help, born in the workhouse, smelling of the cowshed, snores bass and gruff on a couch of straw in a loft in Salt Lake Farm and picks a posy of daisies in Sunday Meadow to put on the grave of Gomer Owen who kissed her once by the pig-sty when she wasn't looking and never kissed her again although she was looking all the time.

And the Inspectors of Cruelty fly down into Mrs Butcher Beynon's dream to persecute Mr Beynon for selling

BUTCHER BEYNON
owl meal, dogs' eyes, manchop.

SECOND VOICE Mr Beynon, in butcher's bloodied apron, springheels down Coronation Street, a finger, not his own, in his mouth. Straightfaced in his cunning sleep he pulls the legs of his dreams and

BUTCHER BEYNON
hunting on pigback shoots down the wild giblets.
ORGAN MORGAN [*High and softly*]
Help!
GOSSAMER BEYNON [*Softly*]
my foxy darling.

FIRST VOICE Now behind the eyes and secrets of the dreamers in the streets rocked to sleep by the sea, see the titbits and topsyturvies, bobs and buttontops, bags and bones, ash and rind and dandruff and nailparings, saliva and snowflakes and moulted feathers of dreams, the wrecks and sprats and shells and fishbones, whalejuice and moonshine and small salt fry dished up by the hidden sea . . .

SECOND VOICE The owls are hunting. Look, over Bethesda gravestones one hoots and swoops and catches a mouse by Hannah Rees, Belovèd Wife. And in Coronation Street, which you alone can see it is so dark under the chapel in the skies, the Reverend Eli Jenkins, poet, preacher, turns in his deep towards-dawn sleep and dreams of

REV. ELI JENKINS
    Eisteddfodau.

SECOND VOICE He intricately rhymes, to the music of crwth and pibgorn, all night long in his druid's seedy nightie in a beer-tent black with parchs.

FIRST VOICE Mr Pugh, schoolmaster, fast asleep, pretends to be sleeping, spies foxy round the droop of his nightcap and

MR PUGH
    Pssst!

FIRST VOICE whistles up

MR PUGH
    Murder.

FIRST VOICE Mrs Organ Morgan, groceress, coiled grey like a dormouse, her paws to her ears, conjures

MRS ORGAN MORGAN
    Silence.

SECOND VOICE She sleeps very dulcet in a cove of wool, and trumpeting Organ Morgan at her side snores no louder than a spider.

FIRST VOICE Mary Ann the Sailors dreams of

MARY ANN THE SAILORS
    The Garden of Eden.

FIRST VOICE She comes in her smock-frock and clogs

MARY ANN THE SAILORS
>   away from the cool scrubbed cobbled kitchen with the
>   Sunday-school pictures on the whitewashed wall and the
>   farmers' almanac hung above the settle and the sides of bacon
>   on the ceiling hooks, and goes down the cockleshelled paths of
>   that applepie kitchen garden, ducking under the gippo's
>   clothespegs, catching her apron on the blackcurrant bushes, past
>   beanrows and onion-bed and tomatoes ripening on the wall
>   towards the old man playing the harmonium in the orchard, and
>   sits down on the grass at his side and shells the green peas that
>   grow up through the lap of her frock that brushes the dew.

FIRST VOICE In Donkey Street, so furred with sleep, Dai Bread, Polly
Garter, Nogood Boyo, and Lord Cut-Glass sigh before the dawn that
is about to be and dream of

DAI BREAD
>   Turkish girls. Horizontal.

POLLY GARTER
>   Babies.

NOGOOD BOYO
>   Nothing.

LORD CUT-GLASS
>   Tick tock tick tock tick tock tick tock.

FIRST VOICE Time passes. Listen. Time passes.
>   An owl flies home past Bethesda, to a chapel in an oak.
>   And the dawn inches up.

>   [*One distant bell-note, faintly reverberating on.*]

FIRST VOICE Stand on this hill. This is Llareggub Hill, old as the hills,
high, cool, and green, and from this small circle of stones, made not by
druids but by Mrs Beynon's Billy, you can see all the town below you
sleeping in the first of the dawn.

You can hear the love-sick woodpigeons mooning in bed. A dog
barks in his sleep, farmyards away. The town ripples like a lake in the
waking haze.

VOICE OF A GUIDE-BOOK

Less than five hundred souls inhabit the three quaint streets and the few narrow bylanes and scattered farmsteads that constitute this small, decaying watering-place which may, indeed, be called a 'backwater of life' without disrespect to its natives who possess, to this day, a salty individuality of their own. The main street, Coronation Street, consists, for the most part, of humble, two-storied houses many of which attempt to achieve some measure of gaiety by prinking themselves out in crude colours and by the liberal use of pinkwash, though there are remaining a few eighteenth-century houses of more pretension, if, on the whole, in a sad state of disrepair. Though there is little to attract the hillclimber, the healthseeker, the sportsman, or the weekending motorist, the contemplative may, if sufficiently attracted to spare it some leisurely hours, find, in its cobbled streets and its little fishing harbour, in its several curious customs, and in the conversation of its local 'characters', some of that picturesque sense of the past so frequently lacking in towns and villages which have kept more abreast of the times. The river Dewi is said to abound in trout, but is much poached. The one place of worship, with its neglected graveyard, is of no architectural interest.

[*A cock crows.*]

FIRST VOICE The principality of the sky lightens now, over our green hill, into spring morning larked and crowed and belling.

[*Slow bell notes.*]

FIRST VOICE Who pulls the townhall bellrope but blind Captain Cat? One by one, the sleepers are rung out of sleep this one morning as every morning. And soon you shall see the chimneys' slow upflying snow as Captain Cat, in sailor's cap and seaboots, announces today with his loud get-out-of-bed bell.

SECOND VOICE The Reverend Eli Jenkins, in Bethesda House, gropes out of bed into his preacher's black, combs back his bard's white hair, forgets to wash, pads barefoot downstairs, opens the front door, stands in the doorway and, looking out at the day and up at the eternal hill,

17

and hearing the sea break and the gab of birds, remembers his own verses and tells them, softly, to empty Coronation Street that is rising and raising its blinds.

REV. ELI JENKINS

> Dear Gwalia! I know there are
> Towns lovelier than ours,
> And fairer hills and loftier far,
> And groves more full of flowers.
>
> And boskier woods more blithe with spring
> And bright with birds' adorning,
> And sweeter bards than I to sing
> Their praise this beauteous morning.
>
> By Cader Idris, tempest-torn,
> Or Moel y Wyddfa's glory,
> Carnedd Llewelyn beauty born,
> Plinlimmon old in story,
>
> By mountains where King Arthur dreams,
> By Penmaen Mawr defiant,
> *Llareggug Hill* a molehill seems,
> A pygmy to a giant.
>
> By Sawdde, Senni, Dovey, Dee,
> Edw, Eden, Aled, all,
> Taff and Towy broad and free,
> Llyfnant with its waterfall,
>
> Claerwen, Cleddau, Dulas, Daw,
> Ely, Gwili, Ogwr, Nedd,
> Small is our *River Dewi*, Lord,
> A baby on a rushy bed.
>
> By Carreg Cennen, King of time,
> Our *Heron Head* is only
> A bit of stone with seaweed spread
> Where gulls come to be lonely

A tiny dingle is *Milk Wood*
By Golden Grove 'neath Grongar,
But let me choose and oh! I should
Love all my life and longer

To stroll among our trees and stray
In Goosegog Lane, on Donkey Down,
And hear the Dewi sing all day,
And never, never leave the town.

SECOND VOICE The Reverend Jenkins closes the front door. His morning service is over.

[*Slow bell notes.*]

FIRST VOICE Now, woken at last by the out-of-bed-sleepy-head-Polly-put-the-kettle-on townhall bell, Lily Smalls, Mrs Beynon's treasure, comes downstairs from a dream of royalty who all night long went larking with her full of sauce in the Milk Wood dark, and puts the kettle on the primus ring in Mrs Beynon's kitchen, and looks at herself in Mr Beynon's shaving-glass over the sink, and sees:

LILY SMALLS
Oh, there's a face!
Where you get that hair from?
Got it from a old tom cat.
Give it back then, love.
Oh, there's a perm!

Where you get that nose from, Lily?
Got it from my father, silly.
You've got it on upside down!
Oh, there's a conk!

Look at your complexion!
Oh, no, *you* look.
Needs a bit of make-up.
Needs a veil.
Oh, there's glamour!

Where you get that smile, Lil?
Never you mind, girl.
Nobody loves you.
That's what *you* think.

Who is it loves you?
Shan't tell.
Come on, Lily.
Cross your heart, then?
Cross my heart.

FIRST VOICE And very softly, her lips almost touching her reflection, she breathes the name and clouds the shaving-glass.

MRS BEYNON [*Loudly, from above*]
  Lily!
LILY SMALLS [*Loudly*]
  Yes, mum . . .
MRS BEYNON
  Where's my tea, girl?
LILY SMALLS
  [*Softly*] Where d'you think? In the cat-box?
  [*Loudly*] Coming up, mum . . .

FIRST VOICE Mr Pugh, in the School House opposite, takes up the morning tea to Mrs Pugh, and whispers on the stairs:

MR PUGH
  Here's your arsenic, dear.
  And your weedkiller biscuit.
  I've throttled your parakeet.
  I've spat in the vases.
  I've put cheese in the mouseholes.
  Here's your . . .
  [*Door creaks open*]
                . . . nice tea, dear.
MRS PUGH
  Too much sugar.

MR PUGH

You haven't tasted it yet, dear.

MRS PUGH

Too much milk, then. Has Mr Jenkins said his poetry?

MR PUGH

Yes, dear.

MRS PUGH

Then it's time to get up. Give me my glasses. No, not my *reading* glasses, I want to look *out*. I want to see

SECOND VOICE Lily Smalls the treasure down on her red knees washing the front step.

MRS PUGH

She's tucked her dress in her bloomers – oh, the baggage!

SECOND VOICE P.C. Atilla Rees, ox-broad, barge-booted, stomping out of Handcuff House in a heavy beef-red huff, black-browed under his damp helmet ...

MRS PUGH

He's going to arrest Polly Garter, mark my words.

MR PUGH

What for, my dear?

MRS PUGH

For having babies.

SECOND VOICE ... and lumbering down towards the strand to see that the sea is still there.

FIRST VOICE Mary Ann the Sailors, opening her bedroom window above the taproom and calling out to the heavens:

MARY ANN THE SAILORS

I'm eighty five years three months and a day!

MRS PUGH

I will say this for her, she never makes a mistake.

FIRST VOICE Organ Morgan at his bedroom window playing chords on the sill to the morning fishwife gulls who, heckling over Donkey Street, observe:

DAI BREAD

Me, Dai Bread, hurrying to the bakery, pushing in my shirt-tails, buttoning my waistcoat, ping goes a button, why can't they sew them, no time for breakfast, nothing for breakfast, there's wives for you . . .

MRS DAI BREAD ONE

Me, Mrs Dai Bread One, capped and shawled and no old corset, nice to be comfy, nice to be nice, clogging on the cobbles to stir up a neighbour. Oh, Mrs Sarah, can you spare a loaf, love? Dai Bread forgot the bread. There's a lovely morning! How's your boils this morning? Isn't that good news, now, it's a change to sit down. Ta, Mrs Sarah.

MRS DAI BREAD TWO

Me, Mrs Dai Bread Two, gypsied to kill in a silky scarlet petticoat above my knees, dirty pretty knees, see my body through my petticoat brown as a berry, high heel shoes with one heel missing, tortoiseshell comb in my bright black slinky hair, nothing else at all on but a dab of scent, lolling gaudy at the doorway, tell your fortune in the tea-leaves, scowling at the sunshine, lighting up my pipe.

LORD CUT-GLASS

Me, Lord Cut-Glass, in an old frock-coat belonged to Eli Jenkins and a pair of postman's trousers from Bethesda Jumble, running out of doors to empty slops – mind there, Rover! – and then running in again, tick tock.

NOGOOD BOYO

Me, Nogood Boyo, up to no good in the wash-house.

MISS PRICE

Me, Miss Price, in my pretty print housecoat, deft at the clothesline, natty as a jenny-wren, then pit-pat back to my egg in its cosy, my crisp toast-fingers, my homemade plum and butterpat.

POLLY GARTER

Me, Polly Garter, under the washing line, giving the breast in the garden to my bonny new baby. Nothing grows in our garden, only washing. And babies. And where's their fathers live, my love? Over the hills and far away. You're looking up at me now. I know what you're thinking, you poor little milky creature. You're thinking, you're no better than you should be, Polly, and that's good enough for me. Oh, isn't life a terrible thing, thank God?

[*Single long note held by Welsh male voices.*]

FIRST VOICE Now frying-pans spit, kettles and cats purr in the kitchens. The town smells of seaweed and breakfast all the way down from Bay View, where Mrs Ogmore-Pritchard, in smock and turban, big-besomed to engage the dust, picks at her starchless bread and sips lemonrind tea, to Bottom Cottage, where Mr Waldo, in bowler and bib, gobbles his bubble-and-squeak and kippers and swigs from the saucebottle. Mary Ann the Sailors

MARY ANN THE SAILORS

praises the Lord who made porridge.

FIRST VOICE Mr Pugh

MR PUGH

remembers ground glass as he juggles his omelette.

FIRST VOICE Mrs Pugh

MRS PUGH

nags the salt-cellar.

FIRST VOICE Willy Nilly postman

WILLY NILLY

downs his last bucket of black brackish tea and rumbles out bandy to the clucking back where the hens twitch and grieve for their tea-soaked sops.

FIRST VOICE Mrs Willy Nilly

MRS WILLY NILLY
>full of tea to her double-chinned brim broods and bubbles over her coven of kettles on the hissing hot range always ready to steam open the mail.

SECOND VOICE The Reverend Eli Jenkins

REV. ELI JENKINS
>finds a rhyme and dips his pen in his cocoa.

SECOND VOICE Lord Cut-Glass in his ticking kitchen

LORD CUT-GLASS
>scampers from clock to clock, a bunch of clock-keys in one hand, a fish-head in the other.

FIRST VOICE Captain Cat in his galley

CAPTAIN CAT
>blind and fine-fingered savours his sea-fry.

FIRST VOICE Mr and Mrs Cherry Owen, in their Donkey Street room that is bedroom, parlour, kitchen, and scullery, sit down to last night's supper of onions boiled in their overcoats and broth of spuds and baconrind and leeks and bones.

MRS CHERRY OWEN
>See that smudge on the wall by the picture of Auntie Blossom? That's where you threw the sago.
>*[Cherry Owen laughs with delight.]*
>You only missed me by a inch.

CHERRY OWEN
>I always miss Auntie Blossom too.

MRS CHERRY OWEN
>Remember last night? In you reeled, my boy, as drunk as a deacon with a big wet bucket and a fish-frail full of stout and you looked at me and you said, 'God has come home!' you said, and then over the bucket you went, sprawling and bawling, and the floor was all flagons and eels.

CHERRY OWEN

Was I wounded?

MRS CHERRY OWEN

And then you took off your trousers and you said, 'Does anybody want a fight?' Oh, you old baboon.

CHERRY OWEN

Give us a kiss.

MRS CHERRY OWEN

And then you sang 'Aberystwyth', tenor *and* bass.

CHERRY OWEN

I *always* sing 'Aberystwyth'.

MRS CHERRY OWEN

And then you did a little dance on the table.

CHERRY OWEN

I did?

MRS CHERRY OWEN

Drop dead!

CHERRY OWEN

And then what did I do?

MRS CHERRY OWEN

Then you cried like a baby and said you were a poor drunk orphan with nowhere to go but the grave.

CHERRY OWEN

And what did I do next, my dear?

MRS CHERRY OWEN

Then you danced on the table all over again and said you were King Solomon Owen and I was your Mrs Sheba.

CHERRY OWEN [*Softly*]

And then?

MRS CHERRY OWEN

And then I got you into bed and you breathed all night like a brewery.

[*Mr and Mrs Cherry Owen laugh delightedly together.*]

FIRST VOICE From Beynon Butchers in Coronation Street, the smell of fried liver sidles out with onions on its breath. And listen! In the dark breakfast-room behind the shop, Mr and Mrs Beynon, waited upon by their treasure, enjoy, between bites, their everymorning hullabaloo, and Mrs Beynon slips the gristly bits under the tasselled tablecloth to her fat cat.

[*Cat purrs.*]

MRS BEYNON

    She likes the liver, Ben.

MR BEYNON

    She ought to do, Bess. It's her brother's.

MRS BEYNON [*Screaming*]

    Oh, d'you hear that, Lily?

LILY SMALLS

    Yes, mum.

MRS BEYNON

    We're eating pusscat.

LILY SMALLS

    Yes, mum.

MRS BEYNON

    Oh, you cat-butcher!

MR BEYNON

    It was doctored, mind.

MRS BEYNON [*Hysterical*]

    What's that got to do with it?

MR BEYNON

    Yesterday we had mole.

MRS BEYNON

    Oh, Lily, Lily!

MR BEYNON

    Monday, otter. Tuesday, shrews.

    [*Mrs Beynon screams.*]

LILY SMALLS

    Go on, Mrs Beynon. He's the biggest liar in town.

MRS BEYNON

    Don't you dare say that about Mr Beynon.

LILY SMALLS

    Everybody knows it, mum.

MRS BEYNON

Mr Beynon never tells a lie. Do you, Ben?

MR BEYNON

No, Bess. And now I am going out after the corgis, with my little cleaver.

MRS BEYNON

Oh, Lily, Lily!

FIRST VOICE Up the street, in the Sailors' Arms, Sinbad Sailors, grandson of Mary Ann the Sailors, draws a pint in the sunlit bar. The ship's clock in the bar says half past eleven. Half past eleven is opening time. The hands of the clock have stayed still at half past eleven for fifty years. It is always opening time in the Sailors' Arms.

SINBAD

Here's to me, Sinbad.

FIRST VOICE All over the town, babies and old men are cleaned and put into their broken prams and wheeled on to the sunlit cockled cobbles or out into the backyards under the dancing vests, and left. A baby cries.

OLD MAN

I want my pipe and he wants his bottle.

[*School bell rings.*]

FIRST VOICE Noses are wiped, heads picked, hair combed, paws scrubbed, ears boxed, and the children shrilled off to school.

[*Children's voices up and out.*]

SECOND VOICE Fishermen grumble to their nets. Nogood Boyo goes out in the dinghy Zanzibar, ships the oars, drifts slowly in the dab-filled bay, and, lying on his back in the unbaled water, among crabs' legs and tangled lines, looks up at the spring sky.

NOGOOD BOYO [*Softly, lazily*]

I don't know who's up there and I don't care.

FIRST VOICE He turns his head and looks up at Llareggub Hill, and sees, among green lathered trees, the white houses of the strewn away farms, where farmboys whistle, dogs shout, cows low, but all too far away for him, or you, to hear. And in the town, the shops squeak open. Mr Edwards, in butterfly-collar and straw-hat at the doorway of Manchester House, measures, with his eye, the dawdlers by, for striped flannel shirts and shrouds and flowery blouses, and bellows to himself, in the darkness behind his eye:

MR EDWARDS [*Whispers*]
    I love Miss Price.

FIRST VOICE Syrup is sold in the post-office. A car drives to market, full of fowls and a farmer. Milk churns stand at Coronation Corner like short, silver policemen. And, sitting at the open window of Schooner House, blind Captain Cat hears all the morning of the town. He hears the voices of children and the noises of children's feet on the cobbles.

CAPTAIN CAT [*Softly, to himself*]
    Maggie Richards, Ricky Rhys, Tommy Powell, our Sal, little
    Gerwain, Billy Swansea with the dog's voice, one of Mr Waldo's,
    nasty Humphrey, Jackie with the sniff . . . Where's Dicky's Albie?
    and the boys from Ty-pant? Perhaps they got the rash again.
    [*A sudden cry among the children's voices.*]
CAPTAIN CAT
    Somebody's hit Maggie Richards. Two to one it's Billy Swansea.
    Never trust a boy who barks.
    [*A burst of yelping crying.*]
    Right again! That's Billy.

FIRST VOICE And the children's voices cry away.

    [*Postman's rat-a-tat on door. Distant.*]
CAPTAIN CAT
    That's Willy Nilly knocking at Bay View. Rat-a-tat, very soft.
    The knocker's got a kid glove on. Who's sent a letter to Mrs
    Ogmore-Pritchard?
    [*Rat-a-tat. Distant again.*]
CAPTAIN CAT
    Careful now, she swabs the front glassy. Every step's like a bar

of soap. Mind your size twelveses. That old Bessie would beeswax the lawn to make the birds slip.

WILLY NILLY

Morning, Mrs Ogmore-Pritchard.

MRS OGMORE-PRITCHARD

Good morning, postman.

WILLY NILLY

Here's a letter for you with stamped and addressed envelope enclosed, all the way from Builth Wells. A gentleman wants to study birds and can he have accommodation for two weeks and a bath vegetarian.

MRS OGMORE-PRITCHARD

No.

WILLY NILLY [*Persuasively*]

You wouldn't know he was in the house, Mrs Ogmore-Pritchard. He'd be out in the mornings at the bang of dawn with his bag of breadcrumbs and his little telescope . . .

MRS OGMORE-PRITCHARD

And come home at all hours covered with feathers. I don't want persons in my *nice clean* rooms breathing all over the chairs . . .

WILLY NILLY

Cross my heart, he won't breathe . . .

MRS OGMORE-PRITCHARD

and putting their feet on my carpets and sneezing on my china and sleeping in my sheets . . .

WILLY NILLY

He only wants a *single* bed, Mrs Ogmore-Pritchard.

[*Door slams.*]

CAPTAIN CAT [*Softly*]

And back she goes to the kitchen, to polish the potatoes.

FIRST VOICE Captain Cat hears Willy Nilly's feet heavy on the distant cobbles . . .

CAPTAIN CAT

One, two, three, four, five . . . That's Mrs Rose-Cottage. What's

today? Today she gets the letter from her sister in Gorslas.
How's the twins' teeth?

He's stopping at School House.

WILLY NILLY

Morning, Mrs Pugh. Mrs Ogmore-Pritchard won't have a
gentleman in from Builth Wells because he'll sleep in her sheets,
Mrs Rose-Cottage's sister in Gorslas's twins have got to have
them out . . .

MRS PUGH

Give me the parcel.

WILLY NILLY

It's for *Mr* Pugh, Mrs Pugh.

MRS PUGH

Never you mind. What's inside it?

WILLY NILLY

A book called 'Lives of the Great Poisoners'.

CAPTAIN CAT

That's Manchester House.

WILLY NILLY

Morning, Mr Edwards. Very small news. Mrs Ogmore-Pritchard
won't have birds in the house, and Mr Pugh's bought a book
now on how to do in Mrs Pugh.

MR EDWARDS

Have you got a letter from *her*?

WILLY NILLY

Miss Price loves you with all her heart. Smelling of lavender
today. She's down to the last of the elderflower wine but the
quince jam's bearing up and she's knitting roses on the doilies.
Last week she sold three jars of boiled sweets, pound of
humbugs, half a box of jellybabies and six coloured photos of
Llareggub. Yours for ever. Then twenty-one X's.

MR EDWARDS

Oh, Willy Nilly, she's a ruby! Here's my letter. Put it into her
hands now.

FIRST VOICE Down the street comes Willy Nilly. And Captain Cat hears other steps approaching.

CAPTAIN CAT

Mr Waldo hurrying to the Sailors' Arms. Pint of stout with an egg in it.

[*Softly*] There's a letter for him.

WILLY NILLY

It's another paternity summons, Mr Waldo.

FIRST VOICE The quick footsteps hurry on along the cobbles and up three steps to the Sailors' Arms.

MR WALDO [*Calling out*]

Quick, Sinbad. Pint of stout. And no egg in.

FIRST VOICE People are moving, now, up and down the cobbled street.

CAPTAIN CAT

All the women are out this morning, in the sun. You can tell it's Spring. There goes Mrs Cherry, you can tell her by her trotters, off she trots new as a daisy. Who's that talking by the pump? Mrs Floyd and Boyo, talking flatfish. What can you talk about flatfish? That's Mrs Dai Bread One, waltzing up the street like a jelly, every time she shakes it's slap slap slap. Who's that? Mrs Butcher Beynon with her pet black cat, it follows her everywhere, miaow and all. There goes Mrs Twenty Three, important, the sun gets up and goes down in her dewlap, when she shuts her eyes, it's night. High heels now, in the morning too, Mrs Rose-Cottage's eldest, Mae, seventeen and never been kissed ho ho, going young and milking under my window to the field with the nannygoats, she reminds me all the way. Can't hear what the women are gabbing round the pump. Same as ever. Who's having a baby, who blacked whose eye, seen Polly Garter giving her belly an airing, there should be a law, seen Mrs Beynon's new mauve jumper it's her old grey jumper dyed, who's dead, who's dying, there's a lovely day, oh the cost of soapflakes!

[*Organ music distant.*]

CAPTAIN CAT

Organ Morgan's at it early. You can *tell* its Spring.

FIRST VOICE And he hears the noise of milk-cans.

CAPTAIN CAT

Ocky Milkman on his round. I will say this, his milk's as fresh as the dew. Half dew it is. Snuffle on, Ocky, watering the town.

Somebody's coming. Now the voices round the pump can see somebody coming. Hush, there's a hush! You can tell by the noise of the hush, it's Polly Garter. [*Louder*] Hullo, Polly, who's there?

POLLY GARTER [*Off*]

Me, love.

CAPTAIN CAT

That's Polly Garter. [*Softly*] Hullo, Polly, my love.

SECOND VOICE Can you hear the dumb goose-hiss of the wives as they huddle and peck or flounce at a waddle away? Who cuddled you when? Which of their gandering hubbies moaned in Milk Wood for your naughty mothering arms and body like a wardrobe, love? Scrub the floors of the Welfare Hall for the Mothers' Union Social Dance, you're one mother won't wriggle her roly poly bum or pat her fat little buttery foot in that wedding-ringed holy tonight though the waltzing breadwinners snatched from the cosy smoke of the Sailors' Arms will grizzle and mope.

[*A cock crows.*]

CAPTAIN CAT

Too late, cock, too late,

SECOND VOICE for the town's half over with its morning. The morning's busy as bees.

[*Out background organ music.*]

FIRST VOICE There's the clip clop of horses on the sunhoneyed cobbles of the humming streets, hammering of horseshoes, gobble quack and cackle, tomtit twitter from the bird-ounced boughs, braying on Donkey Down. Bread is baking, pigs are grunting, chop goes the butcher, milk churns bell, tills ring, sheep cough, dogs shout, saws sing. Oh, the Spring

whinny and morning moo from the clog dancing farms, the gulls' gab
and rabble on the boat bobbing river and sea and the cockles bubbling
in the sand, scamper of sanderlings, curlew cry, crow caw, pigeon coo,
clock strike, bull bellow, and the ragged gabble of the beargarden school
as the women scratch and babble in Mrs Organ Morgan's general shop
where everything is sold: custard, buckets, henna, rat-traps, shrimp nets,
sugar, stamps, confetti, paraffin, hatchets, whistles.

FIRST WOMAN

Mrs Ogmore-Pritchard

SECOND WOMAN

la di da

FIRST WOMAN

got a man in Builth Wells

THIRD WOMAN

and he got a little telescope to look at birds

SECOND WOMAN

Willy Nilly said

THIRD WOMAN

Remember her first husband? He didn't need a telescope

FIRST WOMAN

he looked at them undressing through the keyhole

THIRD WOMAN

and he used to shout Tallyho

SECOND WOMAN

but Mr Ogmore was a proper gentleman

FIRST WOMAN

even though he hanged his collie

THIRD WOMAN

Seen Mrs Butcher Beynon?

SECOND WOMAN

She said Butcher Beynon put dogs in the mincer

FIRST WOMAN

Go on he's pulling her leg

THIRD WOMAN

Now don't you dare tell her that, there's a dear

SECOND WOMAN
> or she'll think he's trying to pull it off and eat it –

FOURTH WOMAN
> There's a nasty lot live here when you come to think.

FIRST WOMAN
> Look at that Nogood Boyo now

SECOND WOMAN
> too lazy to wipe his snout

THIRD WOMAN
> and going out fishing every day and all he ever brought back
> was a Mrs Samuels

FIRST WOMAN
> been in the water a week

SECOND WOMAN
> And look at Ocky Milkman's wife that nobody's ever seen

FIRST WOMAN
> he keeps her in the cupboard with the empties

THIRD WOMAN
> and think of Dai Bread with two wives

SECOND WOMAN
> one for the daytime one for the night

FOURTH WOMAN
> Men are brutes on the quiet

THIRD WOMAN
> And how's Organ Morgan, Mrs Morgan

FIRST WOMAN
> you look dead beat

SECOND WOMAN
> it's organ organ all the time with him

THIRD WOMAN
> up every night until midnight playing the organ

MRS ORGAN MORGAN
> Oh, I'm a martyr to music.

FIRST VOICE Outside, the sun springs down on the rough and tumbling town. It runs through the hedges of Goosegog Lane, cuffing the birds to sing. Spring whips green down Cockle Row, and the shells ring out. Llareggub this snip of a morning is wildfruit and warm, the streets, fields, sands and waters springing in the young sun.

SECOND VOICE Evans the Death presses hard, with black gloves, on the coffin of his breast, in case his heart jumps out.

EVANS THE DEATH [*Harsh*]
Where's your dignity. Lie down.

SECOND VOICE Spring stirs Gossamer Beynon schoolmistress like a spoon.

GOSSAMER BEYNON [*Tearful*]
Oh, what can I do? I'll *never* be refined if I twitch.

SECOND VOICE Spring this strong morning foams in a flame in Jack Black as he cobbles a high-heeled shoe for Mrs Dai Bread Two the gypsy, but he hammers it sternly out.

JACK BLACK [*To a hammer rhythm*]
There is *no leg* belonging to the foot that belongs to this shoe.

SECOND VOICE The sun and the green breeze ship Captain Cat sea-memory again.

CAPTAIN CAT
No, *I'll* take the mulatto, by God, who's captain here?
Parlez-vous jig jig, Madam?

SECOND VOICE Mary Ann the Sailors says very softly to herself as she looks out at Llareggub Hill from the bedroom where she was born,

MARY ANN THE SAILORS [*Loudly*]
It is Spring in Llareggub in the sun in my old age, and this is the Chosen Land.
[*A choir of children's voices suddenly cries out on one, high, glad, long, sighing note.*]

FIRST VOICE And in Willy Nilly the Postman's dark and sizzling damp tea-coated misty pygmy kitchen where the spittingcat kettles throb and hop on the range, Mrs Willy Nilly steams open Mr Mog Edwards' letter to Miss Myfanwy Price and reads it aloud to Willy Nilly by the squint of the Spring sun through the one sealed window running with tears, while the drugged, bedraggled hens at the back door whimper and snivel for the lickerish bog-black tea.

MRS WILLY NILLY

> From Manchester House, Llareggub. Sole Prop: Mr Mog Edwards (late of Twll), Linendraper, Haberdasher, Master Tailor, Costumier. For West End Negligee, Lingerie, Teagowns, Evening Dress, Trousseaux, Layettes. Also Ready to Wear for All Occasions. Economical Outfitting for Agricultural Employment Our Speciality. Wardrobes Bought. Among Our Satisfied Customers Ministers of Religion and J.P.'s. Fittings by Appointment. Advertising Weekly in the Twll Bugle. Beloved Myfanwy Price my Bride in Heaven,

MOG EDWARDS

> I love you until Death do us part and then we shall be together for ever and ever. A new parcel of ribbons has come from Carmarthen today all the colours in the rainbow. I wish I could tie a ribbon in your hair a white one but it cannot be. I dreamed last night you were all dripping wet and you sat on my lap as the Reverend Jenkins went down the street. I see you got a mermaid in your lap he said and he lifted his hat. He is a proper Christian. Not like Cherry Owen who said you should have thrown her back he said. Business is very poorly. Polly Garter bought two garters with roses but she never got stockings so what is the use I say. Mr Waldo tried to sell me a woman's nightie outsize he said he found it and we know where. I sold a packet of pins to Tom the Sailors to pick his teeth. If this goes on I shall be in the Workhouse. My heart is in your bosom and yours is in mine. God be with you always Myfanwy Price and keep you lovely for me in His Heavenly Mansion. I must stop now and remain, Your Eternal, Mog Edwards.

MRS WILLY NILLY

> And then a little message with a rubber stamp. Shop at Mog's!!!

FIRST VOICE And Willy Nilly, rumbling, jockeys out again to the three-seated shack called the House of Commons in the back where the hens weep, and sees, in sudden Springshine,

SECOND VOICE herring gulls heckling down to the harbour where the fishermen spit and prop the morning up and eye the fishy sea smooth to the sea's end as it lulls in blue. Green and gold money, tobacco, tinned salmon, hats with feathers, pots of fish-paste, warmth for the winter-to-be, weave and leap in it rich and slippery in the flash and shapes of fishes through the cold sea-streets. But with blue lazy eyes the fishermen gaze at that milk-mild whispering water with no ruck or ripple as though it blew great guns and serpents and typhooned the town.

FISHERMAN
Too rough for fishing today.

SECOND VOICE And they thank God, and gob at a gull for luck, and moss-slow and silent make their way uphill, from the still still sea, towards the Sailors' Arms as the children

[*School bell.*]

FIRST VOICE spank and scamper rough and singing out of school into the draggletail yard. And Captain Cat at his window says soft to himself the words of their song.

CAPTAIN CAT [*Keeping to the beat of the singing*]
Johnnie Crack and Flossie Snail
Kept their baby in a milking pail
Flossie Snail and Johnnie Crack
One would pull it out and one would put it back
O it's my turn now said Flossie Snail
To take the baby from the milking pail
And it's my turn now said Johnnie Crack
To smack it on the head and put it back

Johnnie Crack and Flossie Snail
Kept their baby in a milking pail
One would put it back and one would pull it out

And all it had to drink was ale and stout
For Johnnie Crack and Flossie Snail
Always used to say that stout and ale
Was *good* for a baby in a milking pail.
[*Pause.*]

FIRST VOICE The music of the spheres is heard distinctly over Milk Wood. It is 'The Rustle of Spring'.

SECOND VOICE A glee-party sings in Bethesda Graveyard, gay but muffled.

FIRST VOICE Vegetables make love above the tenors.

SECOND VOICE And dogs bark blue in the face.

FIRST VOICE Mrs Ogmore-Pritchard belches in a teeny hanky and chases the sunlight with a flywhisk, but even she cannot drive out the Spring: from one of her fingerbowls, a primrose grows.

SECOND VOICE Mrs Dai Bread One and Mrs Dai Bread Two are sitting outside their house in Donkey Lane, one darkly one plumply blooming in the quick, dewy sun. Mrs Dai Bread Two is looking into a crystal ball which she holds in the lap of her dirty scarlet petticoat, hard against her hard dark thighs.

MRS DAI BREAD TWO
    Cross my palm with silver. Out of our housekeeping money.
    Aah!
MRS DAI BREAD ONE
    What d'you see, lovie?
MRS DAI BREAD TWO
    I see a featherbed. With three pillows on it. And a text above
    the bed. I can't read what it says, there's great clouds blowing.
    Now they have blown away. God is love, the text says.
MRS DAI BREAD ONE [*Delighted*]
    That's *our* bed.
MRS DAI BREAD TWO
    And now it's vanished. The sun's spinning like a top. Who's this

coming out of the sun? It's a hairy little man with big pink lips.
He got a wall eye.

MRS DAI BREAD ONE

It's Dai, it's Dai Bread!

MRS DAI BREAD TWO

Ssh! The featherbed's floating back. The little man's taking his
boots off. He's pulling his shirt over his head. He's beating his
chest with his fists. He's climbing into bed.

MRS DAI BREAD ONE

Go on, go on.

MRS DAI BREAD TWO

There's *two* women in bed. He looks at them both, with his
head cocked on one side. He's whistling through his teeth. Now
he grips his little arms round one of the women.

MRS DAI BREAD ONE

Which one, which one?

MRS DAI BREAD TWO

I can't see any more. There's great clouds blowing again.

MRS DAI BREAD ONE

Ach, the mean old clouds!

FIRST VOICE The morning is all singing. The Reverend Eli Jenkins,
busy on his morning calls, stops outside the Welfare Hall to hear Polly
Garter as she scrubs the floors for the Mothers' Union Dance tonight.

POLLY GARTER [*Singing*]

I loved a man whose name was Tom
He was strong as a bear and two yards long
I loved a man whose name was Dick
He was big as a barrel and three feet thick
And I loved a man whose name was Harry
Six feet tall and sweet as a cherry
But the one I loved best awake or asleep
Was little Willy Wee and he's six feet deep.

Oh Tom Dick and Harry were three fine men
And I'll never have such loving again

But little Willy Wee who took me on his knee
Little Willy Weazel is the man for me.

Now men from every parish round
Run after me and roll me on the ground
But whenever I love another man back
Johnnie from the Hill or Sailing Jack
I always think as they do what they please
Of Tom Dick and Harry who were tall as trees
And most I think when I'm by their side
Of little Willy Wee who downed and died.

Oh Tom Dick and Harry were three fine men
And I'll never have such loving again
But little Willy Wee who took me on his knee
Little Willy Weazel is the man for me.

REV. ELI JENKINS
Praise the Lord! We are a musical nation.

SECOND VOICE And the Reverend Jenkins hurries on through the town, to visit the sick with jelly and poems.

FIRST VOICE The town's as full as a lovebird's egg.

MR WALDO
There goes the Reverend,

FIRST VOICE says Mr Waldo at the smoked herring brown window of the unwashed Sailors' Arms,

MR WALDO
with his brolly and his odes. Fill 'em up, Sinbad, I'm on the treacle today.

SECOND VOICE The silent fishermen flush down their pints.

SINBAD
Oh, Mr Waldo,

FIRST VOICE sighs Sinbad Sailors,

SINBAD
I dote on that Gossamer Beynon.

SECOND VOICE Love, sings the Spring. The bedspring grass bounces under birds' bums and lambs.

FIRST VOICE And Gossamer Beynon, schoolteacher, spoonstirred and quivering, teachers her slubberdegullion class

CHILDREN'S VOICES
> It was a luvver and his lars
> With a a and a o and a a nonino . . .

GOSSAMER BEYNON
> Naow, naow, naow, your eccents, children!
> It was a lover and his less
> With a hey and a hao and a hey nonino . . .

SINBAD
> Oh, Mr Waldo,

FIRST VOICE says Sinbad Sailors,

SINBAD
she's a lady all over.

FIRST VOICE And Mr Waldo, who is thinking of a woman soft as Eve and sharp as sciatica to share his bread-pudding bed, answers,

MR WALDO
> No lady that I know is.

SINBAD
> And if only grandma'd die, cross my heart I'd go down on my knees Mr Waldo and I'd say Miss Gossamer I'd say

CHILDREN'S VOICES
> When birds do sing a ding a ding a ding
> Sweet luvvers luv the Spring . . .

SECOND VOICE Polly Garter sings, still on her knees,

POLLY GARTER
> Tom Dick and Harry were three fine men

And I'll never have such
CHILDREN
Ding a ding
POLLY GARTER
again.

FIRST VOICE And the morning school is over, and Captain Cat at his curtained schooner's porthole open to the Spring sun tides hears the naughty forfeiting children tumble and rhyme on the cobbles . . .

GIRLS' VOICES
Gwennie call the boys
They make such a noise.
GIRL
Boys boys boys
Come along to me.
GIRLS' VOICES
Boys boys boys
Kiss Gwennie where she says
Or give her a penny.
Go on, Gwennie.
GIRL
Kiss me in Goosegog Lane
Or give me a penny.
What's your name?
FIRST BOY
Billy.
GIRL
Kiss me in Goosegog Lane Billy
Or give me a penny silly.
FIRST BOY
Gwennie Gwennie
I kiss you in Goosegog Lane
Now I haven't got to give you a penny.
GIRLS' VOICES
Boys boys boys
Kiss Gwennie where she says

Or give her a penny.
Go on, Gwennie.

GIRL

Kiss me on Llareggub Hill
Or give me a penny.
What's your name?

SECOND BOY

Johnnie Cristo.

GIRL

Kiss me on Llareggub Hill Johnnie Cristo
Or give me a penny, mister.

SECOND BOY

Gwennie Gwennie
I kiss you on Llareggub Hill.
Now I haven't got to give you a penny.

GIRLS' VOICES

Boys boys boys
Kiss Gwennie where she says
Or give her a penny.
Go on, Gwennie.

GIRL

Kiss me in Milk Wood
Or give me a penny.
What's your name?

THIRD BOY

Dicky.

GIRL

Kiss me in Milk Wood Dicky
Or give me a penny quickly.

THIRD BOY

Gwennie Gwennie
I can't kiss you in Milk Wood.

GIRLS' VOICES

Gwennie ask him why.

GIRL

Why?

THIRD BOY
> Because my mother said I mustn't.

GIRLS' VOICES
> Cowardy cowardy custard
> Give Gwennie a penny.

GIRL
> Give me a penny.

THIRD BOY
> I haven't got any.

GIRLS' VOICES
> Put him in the river
> Up to his liver
> Quick quick Dirty Dick
> Beat him on the bum
> With a rhubarb stick.
> Aiee!
> Hush!

FIRST VOICE And the shrill girls giggle and master around him and squeal as they clutch and thrash, and he blubbers away downhill with his patched pants falling, and his tear-splashed blush burns all the way as the triumphant bird-like sisters scream with buttons in their claws and the bully brothers hoot after him his little nickname and his mother's shame and his father's wickedness with the loose wild barefoot women of the hovels of the hills. It all means nothing at all, and, howling for his milky mum, for her cawl and buttermilk and cowbreath and Welshcakes and the fat birth-smelling bed and moonlit kitchen of her arms, he'll never forget as he paddles blind home through the weeping end of the world. Then his tormentors tussle and run to the Cockle Street sweet-shop, their pennies sticky as honey, to buy from Miss Myfanwy Price, who is cocky and neat as a puff-bosomed robin and her small round buttocks tight as ticks, gobstoppers big as wens that rainbow as you suck, brandyballs, winegums, hundreds and thousands, liquorice sweet as sick, nugget to tug and ribbon out like another red rubbery tongue, gum to glue in girls' curls, crimson cough-drops to spit blood, ice-cream cornets, dandelion-and-burdock, raspberry and cherryade, pop goes the weasel and the wind.

SECOND VOICE Gossamer Beynon high-heels out of school. The sun hums down through the cotton flowers of her dress into the bell of her heart and buzzes in the honey there and couches and kisses, lazy-loving and boozed, in her red-berried breast. Eyes run from the trees and windows of the street steaming, 'Gossamer', and strip her to the nipples and the bees. She blazes naked past the Sailors' Arms, the only woman on the Dai-Adamed earth. Sinbad Sailors places on her thighs still dewdamp from the first mangrowing cockcrow garden his reverent goat-bearded hands.

GOSSAMER BEYNON

    I don't care if he *is* common,

SECOND VOICE she whispers to her salad-day deep self,

GOSSAMER BEYNON

    I want to gobble him up.
    I don't care if he *does* drop his aitches,

SECOND VOICE she tells the stripped and mother-of-the-world big-beamed and Eve-hipped spring of her self,

GOSSAMER BEYNON

            so long as he's all cucumber and hooves.

SECOND VOICE Sinbad Sailors watches her go by, demure and proud and schoolmarm in her crisp flower dress and sun-defying hat, with never a look or lilt or wriggle, the butcher's unmelting icemaiden daughter veiled forever from the hungry hug of his eyes.

SINBAD SAILORS

    Oh, Gossamer Beynon, why are you so proud?

SECOND VOICE He grieves to his Guinness.

SINBAD SAILORS

    Oh, beautiful beautiful Gossamer B., I wish I wish that you
    were for me. I wish you were not so educated.

SECOND VOICE She feels his goatbeard tickle her in the middle of the world like a tuft of wiry fire, and she turns, in a terror of delight, away from his whips and whiskery conflagration and sits down in the kitchen to a plate heaped high with chips and the kidneys of lambs.

FIRST VOICE In the blind-drawn dark dining-room of School House, dusty and echoing as a dining room in a vault, Mr and Mrs Pugh are silent over cold grey cottage pie. Mr Pugh reads, as he forks the shroud meat in, from 'Lives of the Great Poisoners'. He has bound a plain brown-paper cover round the book. Slyly, between slow mouthfuls, he sidespies up at Mrs Pugh, poisons her with his eye, then goes on reading. He underlines certain passages and smiles in secret.

MRS PUGH
      Persons with manners do not read at table,

FIRST VOICE says Mrs Pugh. She swallows a digestive tablet as big as a horse-pill, washing it down with clouded peasoup water.

      [*Pause.*]
MRS PUGH
      Some persons were brought up in pigsties.
MR PUGH
      Pigs don't read at table, dear.

FIRST VOICE Bitterly she flicks dust from the broken cruet. It settles on the pie in a thin gnat-rain.

MR PUGH
      Pigs can't read, my dear.
MRS PUGH
      I know one who can.

FIRST VOICE Alone in the hissing laboratory of his wishes, Mr Pugh minces among bad vats and jeroboams, tiptoes through spinneys of murdering herbs, agony dancing in his crucibles, and mixes especially for Mrs Pugh a venomous porridge unknown to toxologists which will scald and viper through her until her ears fall off like figs, her toes grow big and black as balloons, and steam comes screaming out of her navel.

MR PUGH
      You know best, dear,

FIRST VOICE says Mr Pugh, and quick as a flash he ducks her in rat soup.

MRS PUGH

What's that book by your trough, Mr Pugh?

MR PUGH

It's a theological work, my dear. 'Lives of the Great Saints'.

FIRST VOICE Mrs Pugh smiles. An icicle forms in the cold air of the dining vault.

MRS PUGH

I saw you talking to a saint this morning. Saint Polly Garter. She was martyred again last night in Milk Wood. Mrs Organ Morgan saw her with Mr Waldo.

MRS ORGAN MORGAN

And when they saw me they pretended they were looking for nests,

SECOND VOICE said Mrs Organ Morgan to her husband, with her mouth full of fish as a pelican's.

MRS ORGAN MORGAN

But you don't go nesting in long combinations, I said to myself, like Mr Waldo was wearing, and your dress nearly over your head like Polly Garter's. Oh, they didn't fool me.

SECOND VOICE One big bird gulp, and the flounder's gone. She licks her lips and goes stabbing again.

MRS ORGAN MORGAN

And when you think of all those babies she's got, then all I can say is she'd better give up bird nesting that's all I can say, it isn't the right kind of hobby at all for a woman that can't say No even to midgets. Remember Tom Spit? He wasn't any bigger than a baby and he gave her two. But they're two nice boys, I will say that, Fred Spit and Arthur. Sometimes I like Fred best and sometimes I like Arthur. Who do you like best, Organ?

ORGAN MORGAN

Oh, Bach without any doubt. Bach every time for me.

MRS ORGAN MORGAN

Organ Morgan, you haven't been listening to a word I said. It's organ organ all the time with you . . .

SECOND VOICE And she bursts into tears, and, in the middle of her salty howling, nimbly spears a small flat fish and pelicans it whole.

ORGAN MORGAN

And then Palestrina,

SECOND VOICE says Organ Morgan.

FIRST VOICE Lord Cut-Glass, in his kitchen full of time, squats down alone to a dogdish, marked Fido, of peppery fish-scraps and listens to the voices of his sixty-six clocks – (one for each year of his loony age) – and watches, with love, their black-and-white moony loudlipped faces tocking the earth away: slow clocks, quick clocks, pendulumed heart-knocks, china, alarm, grandfather, cuckoo; clocks shaped like Noah's whirring Ark, clocks that bicker in marble ships, clocks in the wombs of glass women, hourglass chimers, tu-wit-tu-woo clocks, clocks that pluck tunes, Vesuvius clocks all black bells and lava, Niagara clocks that cataract their ticks, old time-weeping clocks with ebony beards, clocks with no hands forever drumming out time without ever knowing what time it is. His sixty-six singers are all set at different hours. Lord Cut-Glass lives in a house and a life at siege. Any minute or dark day now, the unknown enemy will loot and savage downhill, but they will not catch him napping. Sixty-six different times in his fish-slimy kitchen ping, strike, tick, chime and tock.

SECOND VOICE The lust and lilt and lather and emerald breeze and crackle of the bird-praise and body of Spring with its breasts full of rivering May-milk, means, to that lordly fish-head nibbler, nothing but another nearness to the tribes and navies of the Last Black Day who'll sear and pillage down Armageddon Hill to his double-locked rusty-shuttered tick tock dust scrabbled shack at the bottom of the town that has fallen head over bells in love.

POLLY GARTER

And I'll never have such loving again,

SECOND VOICE pretty Polly hums and longs.

POLLY GARTER [*Sings*]
Now when farmers' boys on the first fair day
Come down from the hills to drink and be gay,
Before the sun sinks I'll lie there in their arms –
For they're *good* bad boys from the lonely farms,

But I always think as we tumble into bed
Of little Willy Wee who is dead, dead, dead . . .
[*A long silence.*]

FIRST VOICE The sunny slow lulling afternoon yawns and moons through the dozy town. The sea lolls, laps and idles in, with fishes sleeping in its lap. The meadows still as Sunday, the shut-eye tasselled bulls, the goat-and-daisy dingles, nap happy and lazy. The dumb duck-ponds snooze. Clouds sag and pillow on Llareggub Hill. Pigs grunt in a wet wallow-bath, and smile as they snort and dream. They dream of the acorned swill of the world, the rooting for pig-fruit, the bagpipe dugs of the mother sow, the squeal and snuffle of yesses of the women pigs in rut. They mud-bask and snout in the pig-loving sun; their tails curl; they rollick and slobber and snore to deep, smug, after-swill sleep. Donkeys angelically drowse on Donkey Down.

MRS PUGH
Persons with manners,

SECOND VOICE snaps Mrs cold Pugh,

MRS PUGH
do not *nod* at table.

SECOND VOICE Mr Pugh cringes awake. He puts on a soft-soaping smile: it is sad and grey under his nicotine-eggyellow weeping walrus Victorian moustache worn thick and long in memory of Doctor Crippen.

MRS PUGH
You should wait until you retire to your sty,

SECOND VOICE says Mrs Pugh, sweet as a razor. His fawning measly quarter-smile freezes. Sly and silent, he foxes into his chemist's den and there, in a hiss and prussic circle of cauldrons and phials brimful with pox and the Black Death, cooks up a fricassee of deadly nightshade, nicotine, hot frog, cyanide and bat-spit for his needling stalactite hag and bednag of a pokerbacked nutcracker wife.

MR PUGH

I beg your pardon, my dear,

SECOND VOICE he murmurs with a wheedle.

FIRST VOICE Captain Cat, at his window thrown wide to the sun and the clippered seas he sailed long ago when his eyes were blue and bright, slumbers and voyages; ear-ringed and rolling, I Love You Rosie Probert tattooed on his belly, he brawls with broken bottles in the fug and babel of the dark dock bars, roves with a herd of short and good time cows in every naughty port and twines and souses with the drowned and blowsy breasted dead. He weeps as he sleeps and sails, and the tears run down his grog-blossomed nose.

SECOND VOICE One voice of all he remembers most dearly as his dream buckets down. Lazy early Rosie with the flaxen thatch, whom he shared with Tom-Fred the donkeyman and many another seaman, clearly and near to him speaks from the bedroom of her dust. In that gulf and haven, fleets by the dozen have anchored for the little heaven of the night; but she speaks to Captain napping Cat alone. Mrs Probert –

ROSIE PROBERT

From Duck Lane, Jack. Quack twice and ask for Rosie –

SECOND VOICE is the one love of his sea-life that was sardined with women.

ROSIE PROBERT [*Softly*]

What seas did you see,
Tom Cat, Tom Cat,
In your sailoring days
Long long ago?

What sea beasts were
In the wavery green
When you were my master?

CAPTAIN CAT

I'll tell you the truth.
Seas barking like seals,
Blue seas and green,
Seas covered with eels
And mermen and whales.

ROSIE PROBERT

What seas did you sail
Old whaler when
On the blubbery waves
Between Frisco and Wales
You were my bosun?

CAPTAIN CAT

As true as I'm here dear
You Tom Cat's tart
You landlubber Rosie
You cosy love
My easy as easy
My true sweetheart,
Seas green as a bean
Seas gliding with swans
In the seal-barking moon.

ROSIE PROBERT

What seas were rocking
My little deck hand
My favourite husband
In your seaboots and hunger
My duck my whaler
My honey my daddy
My pretty sugar sailor
With my name on your belly
When you were a boy
Long long ago?

CAPTAIN CAT

I'll tell you no lies.
The only sea I saw
Was the seesaw sea
With you riding on it.
Lie down, lie easy.
Let me shipwreck in your thighs.

ROSIE PROBERT

Knock twice, Jack,
At the door of my grave
And ask for Rosie.

CAPTAIN CAT

Rosie Probert.

ROSIE PROBERT

Remember her.
She is forgetting.
The earth which filled her mouth
Is vanishing from her.
Remember me.
I have forgotten you.
I am going into the darkness of the darkness for ever.
I have forgotten that I was ever born.

CHILD

Look,

FIRST VOICE says a child to her mother as they pass by the window of Schooner House,

CHILD

Captain Cat is crying,

FIRST VOICE Captain Cat is crying,

CAPTAIN CAT

Come back come back.

FIRST VOICE up the silences and echoes of the passages of the eternal night.

CHILD

He's crying all over his nose,

FIRST VOICE says the child. Mother and child move on down the street.

CHILD

He's got a nose like strawberries,

FIRST VOICE the child says; and then she forgets him too. She sees in the still middle of the bluebagged bay Nogood Boyo fishing from the Zanzibar.

CHILD

Nogood Boyo gave me three pennies yesterday but I wouldn't,

FIRST VOICE the child tells her mother.

SECOND VOICE Boyo catches a whalebone corset. It is all he has caught all day.

NOGOOD BOYO

Bloody funny fish!

SECOND VOICE Mrs Dai Bread Two gypsies up his mind's slow eye, dressed only in a bangle.

NOGOOD BOYO

She's wearing her nightgown.
[*Pleadingly*] Would you like this nice wet corset, Mrs Dai Bread Two?

MRS DAI BREAD TWO

No, I *won't*!

NOGOOD BOYO

And a bite of my little apple?

SECOND VOICE he offers with no hope.

FIRST VOICE She shakes her brass nightgown, and he chases her out of his mind; and when he comes gusting back, there in the bloodshot centre of his eye a geisha girl grins and bows in a kimono of ricepaper.

NOGOOD BOYO
> I want to be *good* Boyo, but nobody'll let me,

FIRST VOICE he sighs as she writhes politely. The land fades, the sea flocks silently away; and through the warm white cloud where he lies silky, tingling uneasy Eastern music undoes him in a Japanese minute.

SECOND VOICE The afternoon buzzes like lazy bees round the flowers round Mae Rose-Cottage. Nearly asleep in the field of nannygoats who hum and gently butt the sun, she blows love on a puffball.

MAE ROSE-COTTAGE [*Lazily*]
> He loves me
> He loves me not
> He loves me
> He loves me not
> He *loves* me! – the dirty old fool.

SECOND VOICE Lazy she lies alone in clover and sweet-grass, seventeen and never been sweet in the grass, ho ho.

FIRST VOICE The Reverend Eli Jenkins inky in his cool front parlour or poem-room tells only the truth in his Lifework: the Population, Main Industry, Shipping, History, Topography, Flora and Fauna of the town he worships in: the White Book of Llareggub. Portraits of famous bards and preachers, all fur and wool from the squint to the kneecaps, hang over him heavy as sheep, next to faint lady watercolours of pale green Milk Wood like a lettuce salad dying. His mother, propped against a pot in a palm, with her wedding-ring waist and bust like a blackcloth diningtable, suffers in her stays.

REV. ELI JENKINS
> Oh, angels be careful there with your knives and forks,

FIRST VOICE he prays. There is no known likeness of his father Esau, who, undogcollared because of his little weakness, was scythed to the bone one harvest by mistake when sleeping with his weakness in the corn. He lost all ambition and died, with one leg.

REV. ELI JENKINS
> Poor Dad,

SECOND VOICE grieved the Reverend Eli,

REV. ELI JENKINS
> to die of drink and agriculture.

SECOND VOICE Farmer Watkins in Salt Lake Farm hates his cattle on the hill as he ho's them in to milking.

UTAH WATKINS [*In a fury*]
> Damn you, you damned dairies!

SECOND VOICE A cow kisses him.

UTAH WATKINS
> Bite her to death!

SECOND VOICE he shouts to his deaf dog who smiles and licks his hand.

UTAH WATKINS
> Gore him, sit on him, Daisy!

SECOND VOICE he bawls to the cow who barbed him with her tongue, and she moos gentle words as he raves-and-dances among his summerbreath'd slaves walking delicately to the farm. The coming of the end of the Spring day is already reflected in the lakes of their great eyes. Bessie Bighead greets them by the names she gave them when they were maidens:

BESSIE BIGHEAD
> Peg, Meg, Buttercup, Moll,
> Fan from the Castle,
> Theodosia and Daisy.

SECOND VOICE They bow their heads.

FIRST VOICE Look up Bessie Bighead in the White Book of Llareggub and you will find the few haggard rags and the one poor glittering thread of her history laid out in pages there with as much love and care as the lock of hair of a first lost love. Conceived in Milk Wood, born in a barn, wrapped in paper, left on a doorstep, big-headed and bass-voiced she grew in the dark until long-dead Gomer Owen kissed her when she wasn't looking because he was dared. Now in the light she'll work, sing, milk, say the cows' sweet names and sleep until the night sucks out her soul and spits it into the sky. In her life-long love-light, holily Bessie milks the fond lake-eyed cows as dusk showers slowly down over byre, sea and town.

Utah Watkins curses through the farmyard on a carthorse.

UTAH WATKINS
    Gallop, you bleeding cripple! –

SECOND VOICE and the huge horse neighs softly as though he had given it a lump of sugar.

FIRST VOICE Now the town is dusk. Each cobble, donkey, goose and gooseberry street is a thoroughfare of dusk; and dusk and ceremonial dust, and night's first darkening snow, and the sleep of birds, drift under and through the live dusk of this place of love. Llareggub is the capital of dusk.

Mrs Ogmore-Pritchard, at the first drop of the dusk-shower, seals all her Sea View doors, draws the germ-free blinds, sits, erect as a dry dream on a highbacked hygienic chair and wills herself to cold, quick sleep. At once, at twice, Mr Ogmore and Mr Pritchard, who all dead day long have been gossiping like ghosts in the woodshed, planning the loveless destruction of their glass widow, reluctantly sigh and sidle into her clean house.

MR PRITCHARD
    You first, Mr Ogmore.
MR OGMORE
    After you, Mr Pritchard.
MR PRITCHARD
    No, no, Mr Ogmore. You widowed her first.

FIRST VOICE And in through the keyhole, with tears where their eyes once were, they ooze and grumble.

MRS OGMORE-PRITCHARD
    Husbands,

FIRST VOICE she says in her sleep. There is acid love in her voice for one of the two shambling phantoms. Mr Ogmore hopes that it is not for him. So does Mr Pritchard.

MRS OGMORE-PRITCHARD
            I love you both.
MR OGMORE [*With terror*]
    Oh, Mrs Ogmore.
MR PRITCHARD [*With horror*]
    Oh, Mrs Pritchard.
MRS OGMORE-PRITCHARD
    Soon it will be time to go to bed. Tell me your tasks in order.
MR OGMORE AND MR PRITCHARD
    We must take our pyjamas from the drawer marked pyjamas.
MRS OGMORE-PRITCHARD [*Coldly*]
    And then you must take them off.

SECOND VOICE Down in the dusking town, Mae Rose-Cottage, still lying in clover, listening to the nannygoats chew, draws circles of lipstick round her nipples.

MAE ROSE-COTTAGE
    I'm *fast*. I'm a bad lot. God will strike me dead. I'm seventeen.
    I'll go to hell,

SECOND VOICE she tells the goats.

MAE ROSE-COTTAGE
    You just wait. I'll sin till I blow up!

SECOND VOICE She lies deep, waiting for the worst to happen; the goats champ and sneer.

FIRST VOICE And at the doorway of Bethesda House, the Reverend Jenkins recites to Llareggub Hill his sunset poem.

REV. ELI JENKINS

> Every morning when I wake,
> Dear Lord, a little prayer I make,
> O please to keep Thy lovely eye
> On all poor creatures born to die.
>
> And every evening at sun-down
> I ask a blessing on the town,
> For whether we last the night or no
> I'm sure is always touch-and-go.
>
> We are not wholly bad or good
> Who live our lives under Milk Wood,
> And Thou, I know, wilt be the first
> To see our best side, not our worst.
>
> O let us see another day!
> Bless us this holy night, I pray,
> And to the sun we all will bow
> And say goodbye – but just for now!

FIRST VOICE Jack Black prepares once more to meet his Satan in the Wood. He grinds his night-teeth, closes his eyes, climbs into his religious trousers, their flies sewn up with cobbler's thread, and pads out, torched and bibled, grimly, joyfully, into the already sinning dusk.

JACK BLACK

> Off to Gomorrah!

SECOND VOICE And Lily Smalls is up to Nogood Boyo in the wash-house.

FIRST VOICE Cherry Owen, sober as Sunday as he is every day of the week, goes off happy as Saturday to get drunk as a deacon as he does every night.

CHERRY OWEN

> I always say she's got two husbands,

FIRST VOICE says Cherry Owen,

CHERRY OWEN
> One drunk and one sober.

FIRST VOICE And Mrs Cherry simply says

MRS CHERRY OWEN
And aren't I a lucky woman? Because I love them both.

SINBAD
Evening, Cherry.

CHERRY OWEN
Evening, Sinbad.

SINBAD
What'll you have?

CHERRY OWEN
Too much.

SINBAD
The *Sailors'* Arms is always open,

FIRST VOICE Sinbad suffers to himself, heartbroken,

SINBAD
> Oh, Gossamer, open yours!

FIRST VOICE Dusk is drowned for ever until tomorrow. It is all at once night now. The windy town is a hill of windows, and from the larrupped waves, the lights of the lamps in the windows call back the day and the dead that have run away to sea. All over the calling dark, babies and old men are bribed and lullabied to sleep.

FIRST WOMAN'S VOICE
Hushabye, baby, the sandman is coming . . .

SECOND WOMAN'S VOICE
Rockabye, grandpa, in the treetop,
When the wind blows, the cradle will rock,
When the bough breaks, the cradle will fall,
Down will come grandpa, whiskers and all.

FIRST VOICE Or their daughters cover up the old unwinking men like parrots, and in their little dark in the lit and bustling young kitchen corners, all night long they watch, beady-eyed, the long night through in case death catches them asleep.

SECOND VOICE Unmarried girls, alone in their privately bridal bedrooms, powder and curl for the Dance of the World.
    [*Accordion music – dim.*]
They make, in front of their looking-glasses, haughty or come-hithering faces for the young men in the street outside, at the lamplit leaning corners, who wait in the all-at-once wind to wolve and whistle.
    [*Accordion music up and down and continuing dim.*]

FIRST VOICE The drinkers in the Sailors' Arms drink to the failure of the dance.

FIRST DRINKER
    Down with the waltzing and skipping.
SECOND DRINKER
    Dancing isn't natural,

FIRST VOICE righteously says Cherry Owen who has just downed seventeen pints of flat, warm, thin, Welsh, bitter beer.

SECOND VOICE A farmer's lantern glimmers, a spark on Llareggub hillside.

FIRST VOICE Llareggub Hill, writes the Reverend Jenkins in his poem-room, that mystic tumulus, the memorial of peoples that dwelt in the region of Llareggub before the Celts left the Land of Summer and where the old wizards made themselves a wife out of flowers.

    [*Accordion music out.*]

SECOND VOICE Mr Waldo, in his corner of the Sailors' Arms, sings

MR WALDO
    In Pembroke City when I was young
    I lived by the Castle Keep
    Sixpence a week was my wages
    For working for the chimbley sweep.

Six cold pennies he gave me
Not a farthing more or less
And all the fare I could afford
Was parsnip gin and watercress.

I did not need a knife and fork
Or a bib up to my chin
To dine on a dish of watercress
And a jug of parsnip gin.

Did you ever hear a growing boy
To live so cruel cheap
On grub that has no flesh and bones
And liquor that makes you weep?

Sweep sweep chimbley sweep,
I wept through Pembroke City
Poor and barefoot in the snow
Till a kind young woman took pity.

Poor little chimbley sweep she said
Black as the ace of spades
Oh nobody's swept my chimbley
Since my husband went his ways.

Come and sweep my chimbley
Come and sweep my chimbley
She sighed to me with a blush
Come and sweep my chimbley
Come and sweep my chimbley
Bring along your chimbley brush!

FIRST VOICE Blind Captain Cat climbs into his bunk. Like a cat, he sees in the dark. Through the voyages of his tears, he sails to see the dead.

CAPTAIN CAT
Dancing Williams!

FIRST DROWNED
> Still dancing.

CAPTAIN CAT
> Jonah Jarvis.

THIRD DROWNED
> Still.

FIRST VOICE Curly Bevan's skull.

ROSIE PROBERT
> Rosie, with God. She has forgotten dying.

FIRST VOICE The dead come out in their Sunday best.

SECOND VOICE Listen to the night breaking.

FIRST VOICE Organ Morgan goes to chapel to play the organ. He plays alone at night to anyone who will listen: lovers, revellers, the silent dead, tramps or sheep. He sees Bach lying on a tombstone.

ORGAN MORGAN
> Johann Sebastian!

CHERRY OWEN [*Drunkenly*]
> Who?

ORGAN MORGAN
> Johann Sebastian mighty Bach. Oh, Bach, fach.

CHERRY OWEN
> To hell with you,

FIRST VOICE says Cherry Owen who is resting on the tombstone on his way home.

Mr Mog Edwards and Miss Myfanwy Price happily apart from one another at the top and the sea-end of the town write their everynight letters of love and desire. In the warm White Book of Llareggub you will find the little maps of the islands of their contentment.

MYFANWY PRICE
> Oh, my Mog, I am yours for ever.

FIRST VOICE And she looks around with pleasure at her own neat neverdull room which Mr Mog Edwards will never enter.

MOG EDWARDS
    Come to my arms, Myfanwy.

FIRST VOICE And he hugs his lovely money to his own heart.

And Mr Waldo drunk in Milk Wood hugs his lovely Polly Garter under the eyes and rattling tongues of the neighbours and the birds, and he does not care. He smacks his live red lips.

But it is not his name that Polly Garter whispers as she lies under the oak and loves him back. Six feet deep that name sings in the cold earth.

POLLY GARTER [*Sings*]
    But I always think as we tumble into bed
    Of little Willy Wee who is dead, dead, dead.

FIRST VOICE The thin night darkens. A breeze from the creased water sighs the streets close under Milk waking Wood. The Wood, whose every tree-foot's cloven in the black glad sight of the hunters of lovers, that is a God-built garden to Mary Ann the Sailors who knows there is Heaven on earth and the chosen people of His kind fire in Llareggub's land, that is the fairday farmhands' wantoning ignorant chapel of bride-beds, and, to the Reverend Eli Jenkins, a greenleaved sermon on the innocence of men, the suddenly wind-shaken wood springs awake for the second dark time this one Spring day.

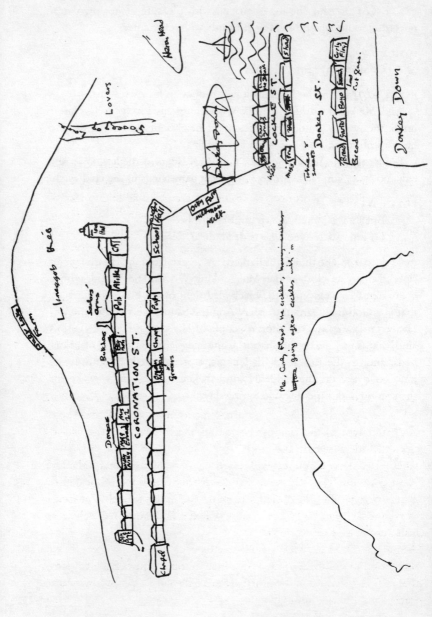

Notes

Under Milk Wood (title): In the early 1950s the play was called 'Llareggub Hill' or 'Llareggub', but Thomas came to feel that the joke in that word was 'a small and childish one' and 'too thick and forbidding to attract American audiences'. Its present title probably reflects the way in which Laugharne (the main inspiration for the village) lies 'under' Sir John's Hill, a wooded headland on which cows graze. But *Under Milk Wood* is also a version of pastoral and the title echoes the phrase from Amiens' song in Shakespeare's *As You Like It* – 'Under the greenwood tree', also used by Thomas Hardy as the title of a novel.

A Play for Voices (subtitle): The term seems to have been Thomas's own idea, though he never incorporated it in manuscript. In a letter of October 1951 to Marguerite Caetani, editor of *Botteghe Oscure*, the Rome-based magazine where the first half of the play was published in April 1952, Thomas called it 'an impression for voices'.

To begin at the beginning (p. 1): Cf. Dickens's *A Tale of Two Cities* (Bk 2, ch. 15): 'Commence . . . at the commencement' and 'All the village . . . withdraws; all the village whispers by the fountain; all the village sleeps; all the village dreams . . .'

sloeblack, slow, black, crowblack (p. 1): A favourite Gerard Manley Hopkins word, 'sloe' (the sour blue-black fruit of the blackthorn) also starts off a typically Hopkinsian paragram – the device whereby consecutive words change only one sound or letter (cf. Hopkins's 'How a lush-kept plush-capped sloe . . .').

dingles (p. 1): Small, deep, wooded valleys.

the shops in mourning (p. 1): An added meaning comes from the fact that in Welsh villages of the time the dark blinds in shop windows were traditionally drawn during funerals.

the Welfare Hall in widows' weeds (p. 1): Welfare Halls were built from the 1920s onwards to provide 'welfare' services such as clinics, recreation rooms, and libraries. They remained an important focus of community life into the early 1950s, when the play was written. After the Second World War many had also become Memorial Halls, dedicated to the dead of two World Wars – another layer in the phrase 'widows' weeds'.

jolly, rodgered (p. 1): The pirate flag (black with white skull-and-crossbones) was called the Jolly Roger. But Thomas's comma also makes 'rodger' ('roger') carry its slang sexual meaning.

anthracite (p. 1): A hard, jet-black coal.

Llareggub Hill (p. 2): 'Llareggub' of course spells 'buggerall' backwards. Thomas's Swansea friend, the composer Daniel Jones, coined for this device the term 'palingram', since 'palindrome' (a word, phrase or sentence that simply spells *itself* backwards, e.g. Napoleon's 'Able was I ere I saw Elba') is a different thing. Publishing decorum in the 1950s insisted that the joke be obscured by spelling 'Llareggub' as 'Llaregyb' – even though 'Llareggub' had been used by Thomas in 'The Orchards' and 'The Holy Six', short stories of the 1930s.

bombazine (p. 2): A twilled fabric, formerly worn dyed black for mourning.

the four-ale (p. 2): Short for a public-house selling four types of ale. In the record of the première reading of the play in New York in May 1953 (Caedmon, LP recording TC 2005), Thomas as First Voice can be heard saying 'four-ale bar' – one of the many temporary 'translations' for an American audience.

with seaweed on its hooves (p. 2): An extra reference is to the tradition that the hooves of mules or horses drawing a funeral cart were padded for the sake of silence. We remember the 'muffle-toed tap tap' of the 1938 poem 'After the funeral', involving both funeral and mule.

coms (p. 2): The colloquial abbreviation of 'combinations', or 'longjohns', a one-piece woollen undergarment with long sleeves and legs.

S.S. Kidwelly (p. 2): 'S.S.' was short for screw steamer or steamship, and the ship is named after Kidwelly, an ancient Carmarthenshire seaside town, across the Towy estuary from Laugharne.

Davy dark (p. 2): The sea has traditionally been called 'Davy Jones's' [i.e., Jonah's] locker'. 'Davy' was a sailoring name for the evil spirit of the sea. But there is also a reference to the miners' safety-lamp invented by Sir Humphry Davy (1778–1829). Thomas also combines the two references in his early poem 'I see the boys of summer' (1934): 'From the fair dead who flush the sea/ The bright-eyed worm on Davy's lamp'.

the long drowned nuzzle up to him . . . (p. 2): Something that may have influenced this passage is the legend of a church and cemetery drowned by the sea in Llanina Bay, near the house that was the poet's home in New Quay in 1944–5. In 'Living in Wales', a broadcast of 1949, he rehearsed the memories that helped keep him in touch with Wales when he was away from home. The list prefigures the details that keep the drowned sailors of the play in touch with life itself: 'settles in the corners, hams on the hooks, hymns after stop-tap, tenors with leeks, the hwyl at Ebenezer, the cockles on the stalls, dressers, eisteddfodau, Welshcakes, slagheaps, funerals, and bethel-bells. What was harder to remember was what birds sounded like and said in Gower; what sort of a sound and a shape was Carmarthen Bay; how did the morning come in through the windows of Solva; what silence when night fell in the Aeron Valley.' The drowned-sailors sequence was T. S. Eliot's favourite part of the play.

Nantucket (p. 3): A whaling island off Cape Cod, Massachusetts, mock-heroically evoking Herman Melville's *Moby Dick*, in which Captain Ahab lost his leg ('lost my step') to the white whale.

Tom-Fred the donkeyman (p. 3): Because of the fewness of surnames in Wales, it has been convenient to identify individuals by adding colloqui-ally a parent's Christian name (Tom-Fred), a person's job (donkeyman), or home (Mae Rose-Cottage), or workplace (Mary Ann the Sailors). The term 'donkeyman' is a reference to the 'donkey-engine', a small engine used to pump water into the boilers of a steamship or hoist freight on board.

sealawyer, born in Mumbles (p. 3): A 'sealawyer' was the naval equivalent of the army's 'barrack-room lawyer' – an awkwardly argumen-tative sailor strongly aware of his legalistic rights. Mumbles is a village on the west shore of Swansea Bay, close to Thomas's birthplace, Swansea.

no my never (p. 3): A Swansea dialect corruption of 'no I never'.

lavabread (p. 4): More correctly 'laverbread', a dish of edible laver seaweed, popular in west Wales. Thomas's spelling reflects the Swansea pronunciation.

snug (p. 4): A small bar in a public-house, offering intimate seating for only a few.

Maesgwyn (p. 4): Literally 'Fair Meadow', a common Welsh name for a farm. There was in fact a farm called 'Maesgwyn' close to his aunt's Carmarthenshire farm at which Thomas spent most of his childhood holidays, celebrated in the poem 'Fern Hill'.

Samson-syrup-gold-maned (p. 5): A reference to the lion trademark for Tate and Lyle's famous 'Golden Syrup', which used the sentence 'Out of the strong came forth sweetness' from the biblical Samson story (Judges 5:5–9), which also includes a lion.

Cloth Hall ... Emporium (p. 5): Characteristic names for drapery and millinery establishments. There was a Manchester House in both Laugharne and New Quay, the two villages that Thomas took as models for the play. But he would also have seen their satiric potential in novels such as Caradoc Evans's *Nothing to Pay* (1930) which has a Manchester House and a Cloth Hall, along with the kind of drapery wares (flannelette and calico) that Mog Edwards lists here.

where the change hums on wires (p. 5): In posh town shops, a system of containers on wires and pulleys was used to circulate payment for goods and returned change between shop-assistant and cashier. The Ben Evans department store in Castle Bailey Street in the Swansea of Thomas's childhood had just such a device.

bottom drawer (p. 5): A young woman's storage place for clothes, linen, etc., bought in anticipation of marriage.

yes, yes, yes ... (p. 5): A comic echo of Molly Bloom's repeated 'yes' in her soliloquy at the end of James Joyce's *Ulysses* – one of several formal and expressive allusions to Joyce's novel.

Jack Black the cobbler (p. 6): One of Thomas's earliest schoolmates recalls that in the Uplands area of Swansea where Thomas grew up there 'was a group of small shops, amongst them Mr Grey the newsagent, Mr Black the cobbler, and White's, the shoe shop. One day, whilst a group of us waited for the school door to be opened, Dylan told us importantly that no one was allowed to open a shop there unless their name was a colour. We all believed him, especially as, by a strange coincidence, the next shop to open was Mr Green the greengrocer' (Joan A. Hardy, 'At "Dame" School with Dylan', *New Welsh Review*, 1995, p. 39). In tribute to Thomas's own sense of accuracy on the actual names of his beloved Swansea, Gilbert Bennett tells me that the newsagent was a Mr Gray, not Grey, that Mr Green opened a sweetshop, not a greengrocer shop, and that a marvellous bonus is that, after Thomas had left the dame school (the period to which this information relates), a tailoring business was opened – by a Mr Brown.

gooseberried double bed of the wood (p. 6): 'Found under a gooseberry bush' is traditionally the feigning answer to children asking how babies are born. But to 'play gooseberry' was also to be a chaperon or an awkward intruder when lovers needed to be alone.

tosspots in the spit-and-sawdust (p. 6): 'Tosspots' were the drunks in the bars of public-houses, which usually had only sawdust as floor-covering.

sixpenny hops (p. 6): Weekend dances in village halls.

Ach y fi! (p. 6): A common Welsh expletive used to show disgust.

making Welshcakes in the snow (p. 6): Welshcakes are traditional Welsh griddle-cakes. The surrealistic picture of Evans the Death's mother 'making Welshcakes in the snow' may also have had a realistic Welsh rural custom behind it. Because of its softness and coldness, and of course the need in hard times to derive water from it, melted snow was used by housewives to prepare their mixture for cakes and pastries.

Never should of married (p. 7): The colloquial Swansea pronunciation of 'Never should [have] married'.

Using language (p. 8): That is, using *bad* language.

Singing in the w. (p. 8): Singing in the w.c., the water closet or lavatory.

Chalking words (p. 9): That is, chalking *naughty* words.

Playing moochins (p. 9): 'Playing dirty', with the connotation of naughty sexual games (from *mochyn*, the Welsh word for pig).

sennapods (p. 9): Dried fruit of a plant, used as laxative.

reformatory (p. 9): A place of correction and training for young offenders.

b.t.m. (p. 9): An abbreviation for 'bottom', but here wittily an abbreviation also of the actual name of the woman ('that Mrs Beattie Morris') with whom Mr Waldo has been 'carrying on'. 'Learn him with a slipper' = 'Teach him with a slipper'.

peke (p. 11): Short for the pekinese breed of dog.

cadenzas (p. 12): A virtuoso solo passage near the end of a piece of music, originally improvised.

Salt Lake Farm (p. 12): One of the best signs that Thomas was specifically thinking of Laugharne is that, overlooking that village, there is a Salt House Farm on Sir John's Hill (shown on Thomas's sketch above, though in the sketch he has moved the hill, called Llareggub Hill, from right to centre-background). In changing 'Salt House' to 'Salt Lake', Thomas went further and named the farmer himself Utah Watkins, after the American state of which Salt Lake City, home of the Mormon faith, is the capital. In a worksheet now at the University of Texas, Utah Watkins is named Mormon Watkins.

Call me Dolores/ Like they do in the stories (p. 14): The young Dylan Thomas once reviewed H. G. Wells's novel *Apropos of Dolores* – in Thomas's words, the story of 'a superlatively common woman'.

Mr Beynon, in butcher's bloodied apron, springheels (p. 14): A reference to a popular Victorian melodrama, *Springheeled Jack*, the title character of which, reputedly based on an actual person, was a butcher given to converting people into pie meat, until a pie was one day found to have a human finger in it. (I am grateful to Mr Terry Phillips for pointing out this source.)

Eisteddfodau (p. 15): Plural of eisteddfod (the word derives from the Welsh *eistedd*, meaning 'to sit'). Originally an assembly of poets, the institution survives as the main Welsh-language competitive literary, musical and cultural festival, at both national and regional levels.

He intricately rhymes, to the music of crwth and pibgorn (p. 15): The phrase 'intricately rhymes' portrays Eli Jenkins as a poet able to employ the traditional strict metres of the medieval Welsh poets. A *crwth* (or *crowd*) was a musical instrument of the lyre family, but played with a bow. A *pibgorn* was literally a 'horn pipe'. Both instruments accompanied traditional, sung Welsh poetry of the 'intricately rhymed' variety. The morning poem Eli Jenkins recites shows some of the consonantal chiming effects of such poetry, but is mainly aimed as a satire on local newspaper verse.

his druid's seedy nightie in a beer-tent black with parchs (p. 15): A concentration of satiric barbs. The main *gorsedd* ('assembly') ceremonies of the National Eisteddfod, the neo-druidic invention of Iolo Morganwg (Edward Williams, 1747–1826) in the late eighteenth century, are conducted by elected cultural figures dressed in white robes. The sale of alcohol is forbidden on the Eisteddfod field, but over the years the main ceremonies have been conducted in marquees which no doubt elsewhere serve more often as 'beer-tents'. *Parch* (here inaccurately made plural, English fashion, by the addition of an 's', and used as a noun) is the abbreviated form of the adjective *parchedig*, Welsh for the religious title 'reverend'. Many of the principals of the National Eisteddfod assembly have over the years been 'reverends'.

under the gippo's clothespegs (p. 16): 'Gippo' was a colloquial term for gypsy. A common sight, well into the 1950s, the Romanies or gypsies travelled throughout South Wales with wares for sale, the main item being wooden pegs for hanging washing on a line.

Lord Cut-Glass (p. 16): When used of an accent, 'cut-glass' denoted an affected upper-class or refined way of speaking. It was a term that Thomas used to describe his own un-Welsh accent, the result of early elocution lessons.

circle of stones (p. 16): A circle of large stones set up to mark a place or area where a National Eisteddfod is held.

The principality of the sky (p. 17): 'Principality' is a word often used for Wales itself. Originally, the two contending names for the street that became Coronation Street in the final play were Principality Street and Dragon Street.

Dear Gwalia (p. 18): 'Dear Gwalia' was a traditional opening in poems addressing Wales as a homeland – including a Welsh poem 'Cân Mewn Cystudd' ('A Song in Affliction') by Dylan Thomas's famous great-uncle William Thomas (1834–79), the Unitarian preacher, poet and Radical leader from whose bardic name, Gwilym Marles, Thomas was given his own middle name of Marlais. Gwilym Marles may have been in some ways an unconscious model for Eli Jenkins.

The mountains of Wales named in Eli Jenkins's poem are as follows: *Cader Idris* (Merionethshire; literally 'Idris's Chair' or 'Camp' – Idris is usually thought of as a giant); *Moel y Wyddfa* (Caernarfonshire; literally 'Summit of Snowdon', the highest British mountain after Scotland's Ben Nevis); *Carnedd Llewelyn* (literally 'The Burial Cairn of Ll[y]welyn', the second highest peak in the Snowdon range); *Plinlimmon* (mid Wales, an anglicization of Pumlumon, 'five beacons'); *Penmaen Mawr* (literally 'Head of Large Stone', a promontory on the Caernarfonshire coast of north Wales).

Of the place names, *Carreg Cennen* is a thirteenth-century castle in Carmarthenshire's Towy valley, and *Golden Grove* is a small village in the same area. This is also the location of *Grongar* (literally 'Round Fortress'), famously praised in John Dyer's topographical poem 'Grongar Hill' (1726).

Thomas names eighteen Welsh rivers. Only three present any problems of identification. *Daw* is probably the river Dawan, in Glamorgan, celebrated in other Welsh and Anglo-Welsh works, for example 'Banks of the Daw' in Iolo Morganwg's *Poems Lyrical and Pastoral* (1794). It comes at a point where Thomas is placing some of the names in alphabetical sequence (a Welsh poetic device called *cymeriad*): hence *Claerwen, Cleddau, Dulas, Daw, Ely, Gwili*. (See the note on 'He intricately rhymes . . .', p. 70 above.) The real *River Dewi* in Laugharne is the river Corran, a thin stream running through the village; but Dewi is also the actual name of a nearby tributary of the Taf, one of the two main rivers running into the sea at Laugharne. The text handed down to us prints Taf (soft 'f') as *Taff* (hard 'f'). Thomas, who did not speak Welsh, probably thought that even the Taf with a soft 'f' was spelt 'Taff' in print. But Taff is normally used of a different river in industrial South Wales. That Thomas meant the Taf, which merged with the Towy in Carmarthen Bay outside his window in Laugharne, is suggested by the fact that he pronounces it with a soft 'f' in the stage reading recorded in New York in May 1953 (Caedmon, LP recording TC 2005).

Mrs Beynon's treasure (p. 19): 'Treasure' in the sense of a highly valued domestic help.

a dream of royalty (p. 19): Writing to his wife from New York, Thomas said that he had finished his 'infernally, eternally unfinished "Play"' and would be flying home on 2 June 1953 – the day of Queen Elizabeth II's coronation.

primus ring (p. 19): A portable paraffin cooking ring.

Welsh male voices (p. 23): That is, the voices of a Welsh male-voice choir.

big-besomed (p. 23): A besom (with a play on 'bosom') is a broom. But 'besom' is also a northern dialect word for a dominant woman.

bubble-and-squeak (p. 23): A meal of leftover vegetables, so called from the noise it makes when being fried.

'Aberystwyth' (p. 25): A famous hymn-tune composed by Sir Joseph Parry in 1877.

the sun gets up and goes down in her dewlap (p. 31): A satirical trope as old as Chaucer's 'Up rose the sun and up rose Emily' in *The Knight's Tale*.

Tallyho (p. 33): According to Thomas's wife Caitlin, her father, Francis Macnamara, 'seemed to make love quite impersonally . . . right at the crucial moment he would shout "Ship ahoy!"'.

sea-memory again (p. 35): The phrase 'sea-memory' is used as an adverb.

jig jig (p. 35): An internationally understood term for sexual intercourse, used by prostitutes in seaports.

late of Twll (p. 36): The joke regarding the tidy Mog Edwards's previous business address lies in the fact that *twll* in Welsh (literally 'a hole') is used of a place that one thinks of as 'a dump'.

'The Rustle of Spring' (p. 38): A piano piece by the Norwegian Christian Sinding (1856–1941), who was ranked next to Grieg as a national composer. Its popularity as a salon piece had made it a cliché of bourgeois musical taste. The joke is that it is here said to represent the Pythagorean notion of the 'music of the spheres'.

little Willy Wee (p. 39): 'Wee Willy Winkie' is a name from a nursery rhyme, and reminds us that that is the form taken by Polly Garter's song.

It was a luvver and his lars . . . (p. 41): The contrast between freshness and false gentility is strengthened by the fact that the song Gossamer Beynon wants the children to enunciate in a more genteel way is 'It was a lover and his lass'. This is the Pages' song in Shakespeare's *As You Like It* (V.3), another play that explores green innocence in a world of courtly presumption and the passing of time.

naughty forfeiting children (p. 42): Refers to a children's game in which a player, on being faulted, has to forfeit a possession or perform some specified act.

cawl (p. 44): A broth of meat and vegetables, a traditional dish in Wales.

pop goes the weasel and the wind (p. 44): The traditional children's song 'Pop goes the weasel' was suggested because 'pop' was the common word for the 'cherryade' and other aerated drinks earlier in the sentence: hence also 'wind'.

salad-day (p. 45): An echo of Cleopatra's words in Shakespeare's *Antony and Cleopatra* (I.5): 'My salad days,/ When I was green in judgement'.

a house and a life at siege (p. 48): Thomas's favourite novelist was Dickens. He may be remembering Mr Sapsea in *Edwin Drood* (ch. 4): 'Mr Sapsea has a bottle of port wine on a table before the fire . . . and is characteristically attended by his portrait, his eight-day clock, and his weather-glass. Characteristically, because he would uphold himself against mankind, his weather-glass against weather, and his clock against time.'

Donkeys angelically drowse (p. 49): The idea of the donkey's patient innocence might have remained with Thomas from the moving translation by Vernon Watkins of Francis Jammes's poem 'Prayer to go to Paradise with the Donkeys', which Thomas chose to read at the Reigate Poetry Club in October 1948.

Doctor Crippen (p. 49): Hawley Harvey Crippen (1862–1910), an American-born doctor, executed in London for poisoning his wife.

What seas did you see . . . (p. 50): The poem crystallizes this, Thomas's own favourite part of the play. A shorter earlier version exists in the worksheets now lodged at the University of Texas. The 'woman' was not identified then as Rosie Probert, and the draft also shows Thomas circling words and images for further attention and development.

> *Woman*
> What seas did you see
> In those (long whale blue sea) days?
> What sea beasts were
> In the wavery green
> When you were master?
>
> Blue seas and green,
> Seas covered with (fur,) serpents,
> And ~~walrus~~ mermaids and whale.

What seas did you sail,
Old whaler, when
On the whiskery ~~pond~~ sea
Between Frisco and Wales
You were his bosun?

Seas green as a bean,
Seas gliding with deer,
And foxes and swans.

And what seas went rocking,
My (apprentice,) my love,
On your (rainbowing) flood?
Cockatoos and (doves)
With (queens) in their pockets?

I am no liar.
The only ~~seas~~ I saw
Was the sea-saw sea
With you riding on it.

the White Book of Llareggub (p. 54): We are meant to think of titles such as the Black Book of Carmarthen, the Red Book of Hergest, the White Book of Rhydderch, etc., the major collections of early manuscripts of Welsh literature and history. Eli Jenkins's single-handed 'Lifework' is comically put in that league. It is emotionally the comic reverse of the nightmare in the 1936 story 'The Orchards', where Marlais wakes from a dream 'more terrible than the stories of the reverend madmen in the Black Book of Llareggub'.

a pot in a palm (p. 54): A characteristic example of Thomas's satire: the palm, that design feature of front-parlour respectability, is ludicrously larger than the pot holding it. In the recording of the original BBC Third Programme production in 1954, Richard Burton as First Voice read from a script where this had been meaninglessly 'corrected' to 'a palm in a pot' (Argo, LP recording RG 21).

Theodosia (p. 55): It is something of a late in-joke that the name of one of the gentle cows should be that of a maternal aunt, whose husband, a Congregational minister, young Dylan Thomas could not abide.

all dead day long (p. 56): An inversion of 'all the livelong day'.

glass widow (p. 56): An ironic pun on 'grass widow', a woman whose husband is not dead but purposely absent.

with tears where their eyes once were (p. 56): Echoing Shakespeare's 'Those are pearls that were his eyes' in *The Tempest* (I.2.399).

the Dance of the World (p. 60): Probably an invented reference to counterbalance the traditional and ever-threatening 'Dance of Death'. The 'unmarried girls' themselves are simply getting ready to go out on dates at the village dance.

that mystic tumulus, the memorial of peoples that dwelt in the region of Llareggub before the Celts left the Land of Summer and where the old wizards made themselves a wife out of flowers (p. 60): A borrowing from Arthur Machen's *Far Off Things* (1922; later included in his *Autobiography*, 1951). Machen recalls that 'as soon as I saw anything I saw Twyn Barlwm, that mystic tumulus, the memorial of the peoples that dwelt in that region before the Celts left the Land of Summer'.

The 'Land of Summer' is what the poet and antiquary Iolo Morganwg (Edward Williams, 1747–1826) called the country he believed was the original home of the Welsh before they came to Britain. He was seeking to render the name Deffrobani (Ceylon – thought to have been the first home of the human race) from a reference in the Book of Taliesin of the fourteenth century.

The idea of making 'a wife out of flowers' alludes to the Welsh tale 'Math, Son of Mathonwy', the last of the Four Branches of the medieval Welsh classic, the *Mabinogi*, where the girl Blodeuwedd ('Flower Face') is conjured from the blossoms of the oak, the broom and the meadowsweet. It is from the same source that Thomas's father derived the name Dylan for his son.

In Pembroke City when I was young (p. 60): Mr Waldo's song imitates the urban broadside ballad, in contrast to the more rural feel of Polly Garter's song 'I loved a man whose name was Tom' and Eli Jenkins's morning and evening hymns.

mighty Bach. Oh, Bach, fach (p. 62): To call the composer Bach 'mighty' is a kind of bilingual joke, because in Welsh the adjective *bach* means 'small'. In the same way, in its second mention, Bach's name is followed by 'fach' – a diminutive term of endearment.